D, AUTOMATED, AUTOMATIC, BABY BOOMER, BABY-SITTER, BACITRACIN, BARBIE DOLL, BEATS,

W-PAY-LATER, CANASTA, CANDID CAMERA, CAPTIVE AUDIENCE, CAR POOL, CERTIFIED MAIL, C
RVETTE, COUNTDOWN, CREDIT CARD, CREST TOOTHPASTE, CRISPER, CUE CARD, CYBERNETICS, DACRON, DAIRY QUEEN, DEAR
AG STRIP, DRIVE-IN BANK, DUAL EXHAUST, DUCK AND COVER, EDSEL, EGGHEAD, EXPRESSWAY, FAIR DEAL, FALLOUT, FALLOUT
D-O-MATIC, FRANCHISE, FREEWAY, FREE WORLD, FREEZE DRYING, FRISBEE, FROZEN FOOD, GERBER BABY FOOD,
CORE, HEADSHRINKER, HELICOPTER, HELIPORT, HOT ROD, HULA HOOP, HYDROGEN BOMB, IBM SELECTRIC, INDUSTRIAL PARK,
UAL-FREEZE UNIT, KING-SIZE CIGARETTES, KINSEY REPORT, KOREAN WAR, KUKLA AND FRAN AND OLLIE, LAUNDERETTE,
LEX, MILTOWN, MINUTE RICE, MISS CLAIROL, MISS FRANCES, MOONDUST, MOONING, MOONLIGHTING, MUSHROOM CLOUD,
OW, IN THE PIPELINE, PIZZA, PLASTIC BAG, PLASTICS, PLAY-DOH, PLAYROOM, PLUTONIUM, POGO STICK, PONYTAIL, POODLE
EE EUROPE, RANCH HOUSE, RAT PACK, RAT RACE, RCA VICTOR, REACTOR, RED-BAITING, RE-ENTRY, REFUSNIKS, ROCK AND
BLE, SCUBA, SECTIONAL, SELF-SERVICE, SEX KITTEN, SHOPPING MALL, SILLY PUTTY, SIMULCAST, SNOWMOBILE, SOAP OPERA,
TO-AIR MISSILE, SWEET 'N LOW, TAIL FINS, TELEPROMPTER, TELETHON, THRUWAY, TIDE DETERGENT, TINY TEARS DOLL, TRAN-
W BUG, WALK/DON'T WALK, WARHEAD, WAX BUILD-UP, WELFARE STATE, WHIRLYBIRD, XEROGRAPHY AIR-CONDITIONING,
ATED, AUTOMATIC, BABY BOOMER, BABY-SITTER, BACITRACIN, BARBIE DOLL, BEATS, BERLIN WALL, BEST-SELLER,
W-PAY-LATER, CANASTA, CANDID CAMERA, CAPTIVE AUDIENCE, CAR POOL, CERTIFIED MAIL, CHA-CHA-CHA, CHLOROPHYLL,
RVETTE, COUNTDOWN, CREDIT CARD, CREST TOOTHPASTE, CRISPER, CUE CARD, CYBERNETICS, DACRON, DAIRY QUEEN, DEAR
AG STRIP, DRIVE-IN BANK, DUAL EXHAUST, DUCK AND COVER, EDSEL, EGGHEAD, EXPRESSWAY, FAIR DEAL, FALLOUT, FALLOUT
D-O-MATIC, FRANCHISE, FREEWAY, FREE WORLD, FREEZE DRYING, FRISBEE, FROZEN FOOD, GERBER BABY FOOD,
CORE, HEADSHRINKER, HELICOPTER, HELIPORT, HOT ROD, HULA HOOP, HYDROGEN BOMB, IBM SELECTRIC, INDUSTRIAL PARK,
UAL-FREEZE UNIT, KING-SIZE CIGARETTES, KINSEY REPORT, KOREAN WAR, KUKLA AND FRAN AND OLLIE, LAUNDERETTE,
LEX, MILTOWN, MINUTE RICE, MISS CLAIROL, MISS FRANCES, MOONDUST, MOONING, MOONLIGHTING, MUSHROOM CLOUD,
OW, IN THE PIPELINE, PIZZA, PLASTIC BAG, PLASTICS, PLAY-DOH, PLAYROOM, PLUTONIUM, POGO STICK, PONYTAIL, POODLE
EE EUROPE, RANCH HOUSE, RAT PACK, RAT RACE, RCA VICTOR, REACTOR, RED-BAITING, RE-ENTRY, REFUSNIKS, ROCK AND
BLE, SCUBA, SECTIONAL, SELF-SERVICE, SEX KITTEN, SHOPPING MALL, SILLY PUTTY, SIMULCAST, SNOWMOBILE, SOAP OPERA,
TO-AIR MISSILE, SWEET 'N LOW, TAIL FINS, TELEPROMPTER, TELETHON, THRUWAY, TIDE DETERGENT, TINY TEARS DOLL, TRAN-
W BUG, WALK/DON'T WALK, WARHEAD, WAX BUILD-UP, WELFARE STATE, WHIRLYBIRD, XEROGRAPHY AIR-CONDITIONING,
ATED, AUTOMATIC, BABY BOOMER, BABY-SITTER, BACITRACIN, BARBIE DOLL, BEATS, BERLIN WALL, BEST-SELLER,
W-PAY-LATER, CANASTA, CANDID CAMERA, CAPTIVE AUDIENCE, CAR POOL, CERTIFIED MAIL, CHA-CHA-CHA, CHLOROPHYLL,
RVETTE, COUNTDOWN, CREDIT CARD, CREST TOOTHPASTE, CRISPER, CUE CARD, CYBERNETICS, DACRON, DAIRY QUEEN, DEAR
AG STRIP, DRIVE-IN BANK, DUAL EXHAUST, DUCK AND COVER, EDSEL, EGGHEAD, EXPRESSWAY, FAIR DEAL, FALLOUT, FALLOUT
D-O-MATIC, FRANCHISE, FREEWAY, FREE WORLD, FREEZE DRYING, FRISBEE, FROZEN FOOD, GERBER BABY FOOD,
CORE, HEADSHRINKER, HELICOPTER, HELIPORT, HOT ROD, HULA HOOP, HYDROGEN BOMB, IBM SELECTRIC, INDUSTRIAL PARK,
UAL-FREEZE UNIT, KING-SIZE CIGARETTES, KINSEY REPORT, KOREAN WAR, KUKLA AND FRAN AND OLLIE, LAUNDERETTE,
LEX, MILTOWN, MINUTE RICE, MISS CLAIROL, MISS FRANCES, MOONDUST, MOONING, MOONLIGHTING, MUSHROOM CLOUD,
OW, IN THE PIPELINE, PIZZA, PLASTIC BAG, PLASTICS, PLAY-DOH, PLAYROOM, PLUTONIUM, POGO STICK, PONYTAIL, POODLE
EE EUROPE, RANCH HOUSE, RAT PACK, RAT RACE, RCA VICTOR, REACTOR, RED-BAITING, RE-ENTRY, REFUSNIKS, ROCK AND
BLE, SCUBA, SECTIONAL, SELF-SERVICE, SEX KITTEN, SHOPPING MALL, SILLY PUTTY, SIMULCAST, SNOWMOBILE, SOAP OPERA,
CE-TO-AIR MISSILE, SWEET 'N LOW, TAIL FINS, TELEPROMPTER, TELETHON, THRUWAY, TIDE DETERGENT, TINY TEARS DOLL,
, VW BUG, WALK/DON'T WALK, WARHEAD, WAX BUILD-UP, WELFARE STATE, WHIRLYBIRD, XEROGRAPHY AIR-CONDITIONING,
ATIC, BABY BOOMER, BABY-SITTER, BACITRACIN, BARBIE DOLL, BEATS, BERLIN WALL, BEST-SELLER, BETTER DEAD THAN RED,

WHEN WE LIKED IKE

Lucien Brown, 1956

When We Liked Ike

BARBARA NORFLEET

LOOKING FOR

POSTWAR AMERICA

W. W. NORTON & COMPANY
NEW YORK   LONDON

Copyright © 2001 by Barbara P. Norfleet

Illustrations used by permission of The President and Fellows of Harvard University.

"Atomic Bomb" by Harold Edgerton reproduced by permission of the Harold and Esther Edgerton Foundation, courtesy of Palm Press, Inc.

The text of this book is composed in Interstate and SignPainter

Manufacturing by Mondadori Printing, Verona, Italy

Book design by Katy Homans

Manuscript editor: JoAnn Schambier

Library of Congress Cataloging-in-Publication Data

Norfleet, Barbara P.

    When we liked Ike : looking for postwar America / Barbara Norfleet.

    p. cm.

    ISBN 0-393-01966-7

    1. United States—Social life and customs—1945-1970. 2. United States—Social conditions—1945-

3. National characteristics, American. 4. Whites—United States—Social life and customs—20th century. 5. Middle class—United States—History—20th century. 6. Mass media and the family—United States—History—20th century. 7. Mass media and culture—United States—History—20th century. 8. United States—Social life and customs—1945-1970—Pictorial works. 9. Whites—United States—Social life and customs—20th century—Pictorial works. 10. Middle class—United States—History—20th century—Pictorial works. I. Title.

E169.02 .N66 2001

                                          973.92—dc21

00-052716

W. W. Norton & Company, Inc., 500 Fifth Avenue, New York, N.Y. 10110

www.wwnorton.com

W. W. Norton & Company Ltd., 10 Coptic Street, London WC1A 1PU

1 2 3 4 5 6 7 8 9 0

Contents

Photographer unknown
Atomic cloud during blast at Bikini
July 25, 1946

Research for this book, and the exhibition that accompanies it, began almost twenty-five years ago when I received a small grant from the National Endowment for the Humanities. This grant enabled me to collect and organize an archive on the social history of America as portrayed in the candid images of professional studio photographers. My interest in this body of work continued long after the grant was over. Each year I try to edit new work. The images in this book, collected as negatives, have not been used in any of my previous books.

I would like to express my deepest thanks to the following professional photographers for donating their negatives to the archive. It is their generosity that makes a book like this possible.

Harry Annas (Lockhart, Texas)
Bachrach Studio (Eastern United States)
Orrion Barger (Chamberlain, South Dakota)
Lucien Brown (Minneapolis, Minnesota)
Robert Burian (Hartford, Connecticut)
Gene Claseman (Sioux Falls, South Dakota)
Sam Cooper (Brookline, Massachusetts)
John Deusing (West Allis, Wisconsin)
George Durette (Manchester, New Hampshire)
Jack Gould (St. Louis, Missouri)
Legler (Chamberlain, South Dakota)
C. Bennette Moore (New Orleans, Louisiana)
Jean Raeburn (New York, New York)
Jack Rodden (Roswell, New Mexico)
Martin Schweig (St. Louis, Missouri)
Joe Steinmetz (Sarasota, Florida)
Frances Sullivan (Derry, New Hampshire)
Lowber Tiers (Vero Beach, Florida)
and
the Harold Edgerton estate, for his print

I thank Suzanne Greenberg, my curatorial assistant, for her help and support in many of the intellectual aspects of the project—from visual and written editing, to research, to making excellent suggestions. With good cheer, long hours, and hard work she has also done many of the routine and exhausting chores that underlie every book and exhibition. Her contributions have been huge and invaluable.

I also thank Allan MacIntyre for making over 500 prints from the negatives. Because we had no funds for this large printing job, he gave us this enormous gift of his time and talent. His suggestions were also helpful.

For their continuing support of photography and the Photography Collection, I am grateful to the many individuals at the Carpenter Center for the Visual Arts: Eduard Sekler, who gave me the chance to organize such a collection; Ellen Phelan, who continues that support today; Chris Killip, who encouraged me to continue working with the collection after I had officially retired; and Chris Frost, who helped with the exhibition and presentation of the project.

Jim Mairs has always had my admiration. With this book I finally fulfill a long-held desire to work with him.

My debts for this book are deep indeed.

Acknowledgments

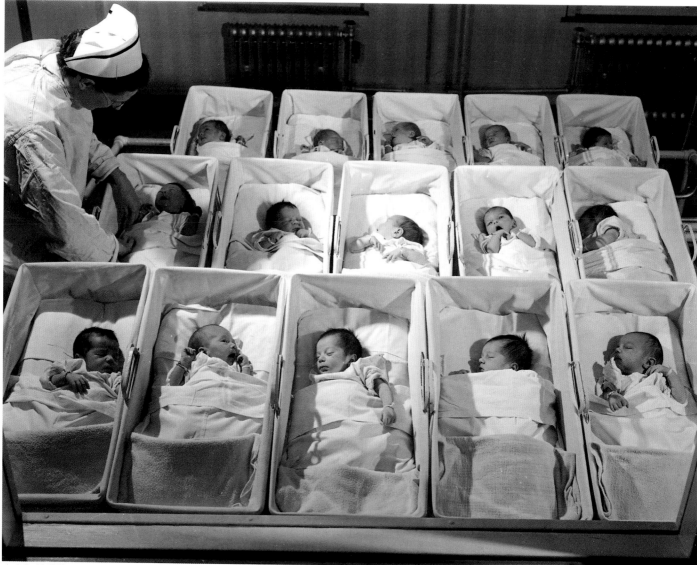

Jack Gould, 1946

In reinventing the period from 1946 to 1959, I realize my memory is contaminated by my imagination, by my changed values and attitudes, and by everything that has happened to me since. We all have a flawed instinct for the reality of the past. But because the aim of this whole endeavor is to get the feel of then, *I have avoided revisionist histories or anything else that did not come from this unique postwar period. All quotations, new words or new meanings of old words, and photographs in this book are from* then.

I remember V-J Day. We danced in the streets, we hugged and kissed strangers. I felt I was part of a wonderful and homogeneous nation, but I was also scared. The war had brought security and prosperity to my family. A gloomy depression town was exchanged for an exciting city. Glamorous older men in uniforms surrounded me. Tennis courts, swimming pools, golf courses, officers' clubs, and dances on navy bases replaced making candle-drip vases out of jelly jars at the local YWCA. My very own bedroom replaced sharing a room in my grandmother's tiny house with my teasing older sister. With the war's end, all this might disappear and we might as a family fall back into being depression poor. I needn't have worried. The privileged time between the Great Depression and the explosive sixties that we have come to define as the fifties brought extraordinary affluence to white America.

A number of the men I had known returned from the war with disease or in great psychological pain; a number had died. I have never understood why I felt so little about loss then and feel so much now when a friend dies. Perhaps I then thought friends were replaceable.

The military men I met all treated me like a china doll because I was so young and my father was their commanding officer. It was also mannerly at that time for all men to treat even older "girls" that way. No females I knew had "gone all the way," but even if they had, I did not know. When Dr. Alfred Kinsey reported in 1953 that 50 percent of married women had had sex before marriage, mostly with the men they did marry, the news took precedence over *Sputnik.* I thought the women had lied.

It was a private time. Friends were told little and parents absolutely nothing, and they wanted to be told nothing, lest they think this child (me) was not perfect and perfectly adjusted. My mother worried only if I wanted to spend time with myself, was not invited to a party, and did not get As in school. I don't understand the last concern because my mother had no ambitions for me other than marrying well. She said the curse of our family was reading. Every book I finished was another step toward spinsterhood.

With the ultimate sex act forbidden, we did everything but. Technically, we were virgins. Deferred gratification made for a most romantic and glamorous time. The songs were mushy, and the petting, always in automobiles, was very good. Men probably felt differently, but I often think that with immediate jumping into bed and "doing it," females are now missing all that tenderness and quite real, sweet sexual feeling and satisfaction that we were told, in an underground way, was okay. "Getting caught" meant getting pregnant, and the term applied only to girls. The assumption was that it only took one to make a baby. I had only one friend who had a baby out of wedlock. She left town.

On the other hand, for a female to go to the movies alone was a sign of total washout. I still can't do it. You hid on Saturday night if you were not asked out so no one would know. It was a time of lies and masks. I learned when to flirt and when not to. I learned the rules of girl behavior—how to be popular, how to pretend I wasn't studying, how to always seem to be having a good time.

The end of the war turned out to be easy on me, but it was much harder on my older sister.

She married a few weeks before her Marine Corps husband was sent to the South Pacific. He returned to find an independent woman and a two year old. The incredible adjustment necessary for both never took place. After four more children, they divorced. My mother did not tell her friends that my sister was divorced for three years. She was ashamed, not for religious reasons but because it indicated a defect in character somewhere in someone.

Robert Burian, n. d.

I went to Swarthmore College. You might think a college with such a radical reputation might have made me political. It did in that the conscientious objectors I met made me, a Navy Junior, into a lifelong pacifist. Unthinkable as it seems today, I thought Stalin was okay. Swarthmore was a nice school where everyone dressed decently; had manners; studied most of the time; had hoot'nannys where we sang Spanish antifascist songs and a few civil rights songs, such as "Listen Mr. Bilbo"; jitterbugged after lunch in loafers and after dinner in three-inch heels with men we didn't date; played bridge; and read, read, read and discussed, discussed, discussed. I fell hopelessly in love with learning, but still one topic for discussion at this very serious college was the best way to hold your head while a man lit your cigarette. Rebellion was drinking too much, wearing jeans, or talking about how you believed in free love — theoretically, that is. During my time there we had our first token African American, but his skin was so light it was difficult to take notice.

I was brought up to believe that women had to trick men into marriage. Not so after the war. Men came back from the war anxious to start a family. That's what returning to normal was about for them, certainly not about returning to the depression of the thirties or the wild twenties. The pressure on those of us much too young to get married was intense. By the time I was twenty-four and had broken off several serious relationships, old-maidship started to haunt me. I almost had my Ph.D., which clearly was going to drive me outside the marriage market, so I finally got married. I found that two could not live as cheaply as one as we began accumulating things.

Then the babies came. There was really no choice about having babies, so having a baby was no special thing — pregnant women smoked and drank martinis and were treated like nonpregnant women. Once those babies were born they absorbed every moment of the day. With my first child, I lived in an unfriendly, incompatible neighborhood where I never really got to know anyone. That baby and I walked the streets all day with my dog. It was a lonely time. Dr. Spock told me I should feel euphoric; he told me that my family would fulfill all my needs. Instead, for the first time in my life, I was tired and wanted to sleep all the time. Was something wrong with me? The baby dominated my life as I tried to maximize his potential, being careful not to be an overprotective "mom."

By the time the next baby arrived we had moved to a neighborhood filled with young people and an endless supply of babies and toddlers. Suddenly the euphoria came and the wonder of babies was real. All morning we mothers got together, drank coffee, smoked cigarettes, and talked about raising children. The children took care of one another. Men were absent. Weekend evenings we had dinner parties—boeuf en Daube, coq au vin, and chocolate mousse. You gave one dinner party and went to two. Women escaped into a nonbaby world and talked about babies. The career-driven men struggled to stay awake. In some miraculous way, all babies, toddlers, and children were in bed by seven and you never heard a peep. Competitive cooking went on in earnest. Dionne Lucas and *Gourmet* magazine were in one hand and Dr. Spock in the other. The best of meals were eaten off doors held up by pipe legs.

No one had much help. Gender functions were rigorously prescribed. *You* were the only one who should raise your baby; *your* child was too important to entrust to anyone you paid. A unique idea in world history. No children have ever been so scrutinized. Kid-watching was a national disease. Moms were obsessed. The children probably longed for private space and fewer toys. I quit my career the moment I tried to get pregnant, as if working would contaminate my eggs.

Babies were indulged, and our houses looked like a chaotic FAO Schwarz. Diapers and toys tripped you in every room, baby oil was in the kitchen. When we moved into a large house in a great neighborhood, the former owners'

Joe Steinmetz , 1949

cook, gardener, housemaid, and chauffeur were replaced by just me. Each baby quickly followed the last, and we all had methods for making a house look baby-free before guests arrived. Mine was to run through the first floor and stuff all of our debris into suitcases.

We never asked ourselves if we could afford all these children. It never crossed our minds that education for the kids or old age for us would be a problem. When the kids were small we were always behind financially and we should have worried, but we didn't.

Don't think for a moment that I let anyone know how I toiled. I was lucky. I needed little sleep, so I continued with the same behavior that had worked at Swarthmore. I had a formula. I was an airhead all day and evening, and then I read, cooked, or cleaned house until three or four in the morning. Did I fool anybody? I don't know. I know that my husband, who knows my habits, is the only person who thinks I deserve any honors I get. It wasn't appropriate then for a female to be seen making a huge effort. I now need sleep and take naps.

It was much later that I discovered that my women friends spent a lot of time on the analyst's couch. I should have guessed this because there were certain set times when you never saw them, and Cambridge, Massachusetts, had as many psychiatrists as it later had lawyers. But it was a time when you didn't tell friends you were being psychoanalyzed.

The only activism I indulged in had to do with my kids. Strontium 90 was getting into their milk and threatened my handsome *Life* magazine family, so I demonstrated against the atom bomb tests in the Pacific and stored up dried milk. Joseph McCarthy became the first TV happening I can remember. We were incredibly passive, but finally everyone I knew, including me, was appalled at his irresponsible ruining of lives and unfounded accusations. We complained but did nothing. I was mentally involved with both Alger Hiss and J. Robert Oppenheimer, but I doubt that I would have been if they had been less appealing—what beauties compared to McCarthy and Whittaker Chambers. One of our jokes was that Eisenhower had died shortly after being elected but that no one had noticed.

TV had few programs so we all shared the same information. We all played Pete Seeger songs to our children. Various friends were going through security clearance, and we took pride in our responses to those FBI and CIA men in their trenchcoats and hats. They stood out like naked people in Cambridge. With serious demeanor we would say when asked that we liked so-and-so but he was too conservative for our tastes.

Orrion Barger, n. d.

My aspirations were to become a gardener at the Cambridge Reservoir when my children were older. I wondered how I would talk them into hiring a woman. A perfect lawn and my neighborhood get-togethers were more important to me than the Korean War, the invention of the transistor, or Jack Kerouac and the alienated Beats. It took the sixties to get me involved in both local and national causes and to even think about racism and poverty and my postponed career. When I finally did start a career, I was flattered when my academic male colleagues (colleagues is too strong a word, for I wasn't treated as one) told me that I was okay because "I thought like a man." My husband felt a huge relief when I went back to work. He was no longer the sole provider for all of us, and I became too busy to be dependent on him for all entertainment. But I also began to have attitudes, especially about the role of women.

History says the mood was intensely optimistic during this postwar period, and it was—at least for the white middle class. I use the word *mood* deliberately because although I was subject to two cases of male violence by strangers I still thought of it as a peaceful time free of crime. I did not report the crimes because I knew I would be told that somehow it was my fault: that I should not be out late at night alone (I was returning from a night seminar), that I should not walk in a lonely spot (I was walking my dog in the woods), and that my clothes were provocative (my jeans were too tight). Not a bad thing happened to me or my children during the 1960s, yet for me that was an anxious and violent time.

Postwar prosperity meant that we did not need to worry. We could concentrate on home, family, and friends, a luxury not shared by African Americans and the very poor, and a luxury that my sons and their liberated wives do not have today as they try to juggle two demanding jobs and small children. They think they missed out on something wonderful. It is hard to convince them that postwar America was a privileged interlude. It was unique. We emerged as the only winner in a war that hurt all the other countries—especially economically. People knew their place, so we were not disturbed by inequalities. The Korean War seemed distant and unimportant. The Beats were more a curiosity than anything else. The cold war fed our prosperity and, after all, our destiny was to save the world from communism. We buried our anxiety about the bomb and the end of the world.

My career may have suffered from those years of domesticity, but it wasn't all bad. The distorted sugar-coated nostalgia for this period is not all distorted and sugar-coated.

The postwar era from 1946 to 1959 does have unity. At the end of the war, America looked very much the way it had in the thirties, but in the cities and open countryside things began changing very fast. In the late 1940s with the marketing of television sets, with transistors, with the magazines *Life* and *Look*, with Jackson Pollock and Jack Kerouac, and with the building of superhighways, the culture began to speed up.

By 1960 a new era began. The first sit-in, the first birth control pill, and the election of John F. Kennedy as president brought the Eisenhower years to an end. *The Feminine Mystique* by Betty Friedan, *Silent Spring* by Rachel Carson, *Unsafe at Any Speed* by Ralph Nader, *The Other America* by Michael Harrington, and *The Port Huron Statement* by Students for a Democratic Society challenged our myths, our self-satisfaction, and our complacency. I hope this work will show why such an explosion was inevitable.

Unlike my memories, photographs may deteriorate but the image does not change over time. The people, places, objects, and behavior did exist. For one instant they were before the lens. Changes in our own lives and times may alter how we see these images and how we interpret them, but the image is fixed. Furthermore, I have taken them out of their original context—no longer are they in family albums, in their correct time and place, or in the daily newspaper. This too will influence how they are interpreted.

Just as these photographs do not lie, so they do not tell the whole truth. This is not an unbiased record of the postwar years. Different photographers from this period have portrayed very different Americas.

The images in this book, taken by professional and commercial photographers, such as Joe Steinmetz and Lucien Brown, highlight the family, rituals, and social events for clients rich enough to hire them. Violence, politics, and war are absent from these photographs. The one photojournalist, Jack Gould, covered daily life and special interest stories, not crime or the daily breaking news. The goal of such photographers was to take photographs that would please. If the photographers were to be successful, they had to understand and respond to the attitudes, prejudices, and values of their clients. They also had to understand the aspirations and iconography of the culture they visually preserved.

These photographers share certain stylistic earmarks and assumptions, such as a desire not to be cynical, ironic, or to catch the subject off guard. They want to portray the subject clearly. They do not use graininess, blurred movement, or extreme contrast between tones as aesthetic devices to portray their own personal vision.

This attitude was in marked contrast to the work of self-motivated artistic photographers working in the postwar period, such as William Klein, Louis Faurer, and Robert Frank, who took pictures to please themselves. These three photographers did not find happiness or community in this period.

The images of William Klein described a postwar America that was unstable, out of whack. It was an America filled with energy and movement, but with an underlying chaos and sense of violence. Louis Faurer captured the visual chaos and anomie of city life. Robert Frank was put off by the American lack of culture; fast food lunches at counters minus linens, the lack of historic ruins, and our insufficiency of tradition disturbed this privileged Swiss male. His images made during this period display a gritty, unappetizing manmade landscape and a sad, alienated people. His view of America is sadder than Klein's and Faurer's because there is no energy, no hope. The work of such photographers and others like them is not featured in this book.

Advertising and other photographs in magazines such as *Life* and *Look* preserved a nation of blond, happy, wholesome white families, a neat rural landscape, and an orderly city. Similar to the Norman Rockwell covers for the *Saturday Evening Post,* these ads promoted ideals about home and private life and the American landscape. This view could not have been more in conflict with that of Klein, Faurer, and Frank, although they all emphasized the triumph of a consumer and materialistic culture. The ads were designed to sell, the art photographers to criticize.

The Family of Man exhibition in 1955 at the Museum of Modern Art, received with an enthusiasm never seen before, emphasized the connectedness and love among mankind and ignored brutality, the effects of poverty, and prejudice.

There are many other photographic visions of postwar America. Ansel Adams, Roy DeCarava, John Gutmann, Clarence John Laughlin, Jerome Liebling, Leon Levinstein, Wright Morris, Lisette

Model, Ruth Orkin, Gordon Parks, Arthur Rothstein, W. Eugene Smith, Dan Weiner, and Edward Weston all interpreted America during this time.

We no longer have the illusion that any photograph is a simple transcription of a reality. Nevertheless these different and often contradictory views of the United States from the end of World War II to 1959 are each a small part of the truth. To find their meaning is not easy. Art photographers take pictures to please themselves. Advertisers make images to sell a product, and during this period they thought the best way to do this was to display the happy family as the goal and purpose in American life. The studio photographers have clients they must please, and they play to the ideals and attitudes those clients hold about home and private life. General interest photojournalists, unlike war or crime photojournalists, find pleasing or interesting events in everyday life to photograph.

Frances Sullivan, 1957

All of these different ways of seeing America include surprises. They reveal more than either the artist or the professional photographers intended. The professional photographers' photographs sometimes surprise us because they do capture racism, poverty, the cold war, the military industrial complex, a desire for progress over concern for the environment, complacency, alienation, self-satisfaction, and materialism—many of the same behaviors and attitudes revealed by Klein, Faurer, and Frank.

The quotations from the social critics of the day that accompany these photographs tell about the underlying tensions in a society that imposed unrelenting segregation on returning African American soldiers, that sent independent women back into recently created and isolated suburbs, that ignored the anxiety about the atom bomb and the cold war, and that did nothing to alleviate the poverty of those at the very bottom of the economic ladder.

Any attempt to describe this period has severe limitations. This book gives four different and inadequate forms of information. The photographs in the book are best at describing the attitudes, values, and aspirations of a white middle class. The social critics are best at describing the tensions and anxieties surrounding this ideal. The newly coined terms and new use of old words from the period are a crutch to memory. The time line summarizes important events.

Reality is slippery and complex. This book will evoke different interpretations and will play to the different memories held by each reader.

Note: With just two exceptions, the photographs in this book are printed from negatives that were donated to the Photography Collection at the Carpenter Center for the Visual Arts, Harvard University. The two exceptions are photographic prints (not negatives) donated to the collection.

Joe Steinmetz, 1949

When We Liked Ike

LOOKING FOR POSTWAR AMERICA

Harry Annas, n. d.

Jack Gould, 1947

[H]ome to Mom, home to the old swimming hole where that delicious mud got between the toes, home to apple pie, home to a man-to-man talk with the soda jerk he used to go to school with, home to remember how he had held hands with Sukie Morgan—or Bildshoff, or what the crap was her name?—under the maples, or elms, or cottonwoods, or chinaberries, or long-leaf pines, or maybe under the water tower by the railroad track, but now he'd have to hurry, darn it all, for he had to make a plane into New York tomorrow morning.

ROBERT PENN WARREN, *THE CAVE*, 1959

Joe Steinmetz , n. d.

What would the member of the village group or small town not give at times for an impersonal setting where he was not constantly part of a web of gossip and surveillance?

DAVID RIESMAN, "INDIVIDUALISM RECONSIDERED," IN *RELIGIOUS FAITH AND WORLD CULTURE,* **ED. A. WILLIAM LOOS, 1951**

I've lived in Peyton Place longer than I've ever lived anywhere. . . . I never want to move away.

GRACE METALIOUS, *PEYTON PLACE*, 1957

Orrion Barger, 1957

Jack Gould, 1951

Frances Sullivan, 1959

Jack Gould, 1956

Jack Gould, 1956

Jack Gould, 1953

Harry Annas, n. d.

Joe Steinmetz, 1959

Jack Gould, n. d.

Orrion Barger, n. d.

Jack Gould, 1957

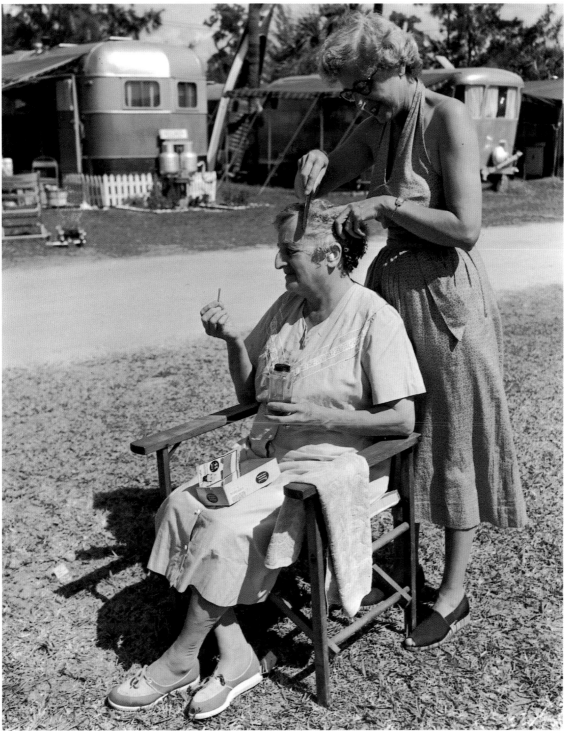

Joe Steinmetz, 1951

Jack Gould, n. d.

Jack Gould, n. d.

"Didn't this used to be Bullard's Drug Store?" "Yes, but it has been taken over by the Midway chain."
FROM THE MOVIE *THE BEST YEARS OF OUR LIVES*, 1946

Jack Gould, 1953

Here I was at the end of America—no more land—and now there was nowhere to go but back.
JACK KEROUAC, *ON THE ROAD,* **1955**

Jack Gould, n. d.

In our modern urban civilization, multitudes of our people have been condemned to urban anonymity—
. . . They find themselves isolated from the life of their community and their nation . . . . This course
of urban anonymity, of individual divorce from the general social life, erodes the foundations of
democracy. For although we profess to be citizens of a democracy . . . millions of our people feel
deep down in their heart of hearts that there is no place for them—that they do not "count."
SAUL D. ALINSKY, *REVEILLE FOR RADICALS*, 1946

Jack Gould, n. d.

Lowber Tiers, 1943

Jack Gould, n. d.

Jack Gould, 1946

Jack Gould, 1946

For most Europeans, the effort to define America, particularly the United States, confines itself to those features which, seemingly, are not European. In that light, the United States becomes some-thing fabulous and monstrous: a place where the entire population lives in skyscrapers, dines in drugstores, works on assembly lines, pays blackmail to gangsters, and exists in a combination of luxury and squalor, or sophistication and infantilism.

LEWIS MUMFORD, "THE AMERICAN IN EUROPE," *COMPRENDRE* **(SOCIÉTÉ EUROPÉENNE DE CULTURE) NO. 10-11, 1954**

Jack Gould, 1946

Jack Gould, 1950

Jack Gould, 1946

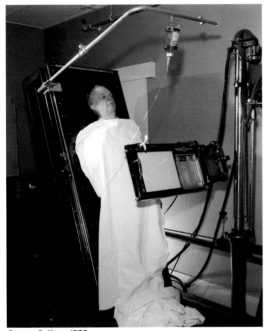

Frances Sullivan, 1958

Frances Sullivan, 1958

The secret of health and happiness lies in successful adjustment to the ever-changing conditions in this globe; the penalties for failure in this great process of adaptation are disease and unhappiness.

HANS SEYLE, M.D., *THE STRESS OF LIFE*, 1956

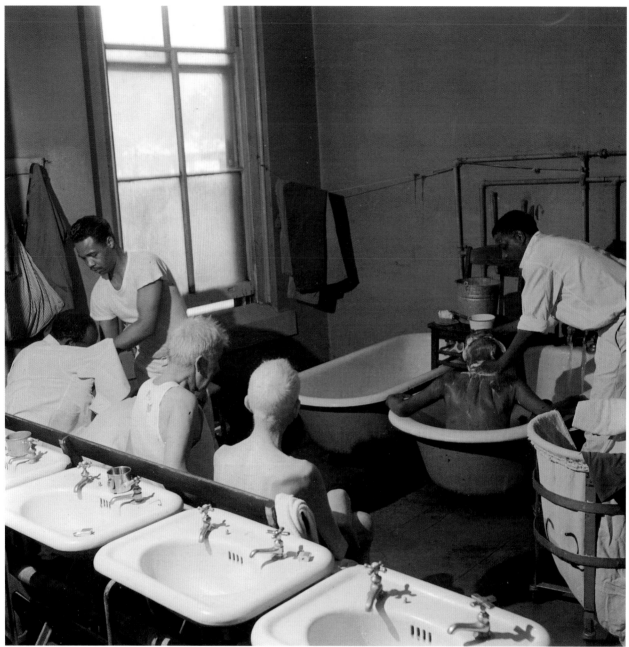

Jack Gould, n. d.

You expect us to give up the old ways, and make this place a little copy of the world outside, the way it's going. I don't say you don't mean well, but it won't do. We're too old and too mean; we're too tired. Now if you say to me, you must move your belongings over beneath the tree, I'll do it, because I have no delusions as to whose mercy we're dependent on.

JOHN UPDIKE, *THE POORHOUSE FAIR*, 1958

Jack Gould, n. d.

[A]ll in the world Mrs. Rogers wanted to do was to go back home and lie down in her own big bedroom in her own big, high-ceilinged house and have Grandma and other members of the Eastern Star come in from time to time to say hello. But they wouldn't let her go home.

JEAN STAFFORD, "BAD CHARACTERS," IN *POINTS OF VIEW*, EDS. JAMES MOFFETT AND KENNETH R. McELHENY, 1966 (WRITTEN IN 1954)

Jack Gould, 1949

Jack Gould, 1957

I had never seen elevators used by children as public toilets. I never imagined that I could find the equivalent of Moscow's newly built slums in the United States. The same shoddy shiftlessness, the broken windows, the missing light bulb, the plaster cracking from the walls, the pilfered hardware, the cold, drafty corridors, the door on sagging hinges, the acid smell of sweat and cabbage, the ragged children, the plaintive women, the playgrounds that are seas of muddy clay, the bruised and battered trees, the ragged clumps of grass, the planned absence of art, beauty or taste, the gigantic masses of brick, of concrete, of asphalt, the inhuman genius with which our know-how has been perverted to create human cesspools worse than those of yesterday.

HARRISON E. SALISBURY, *THE SHOOK-UP GENERATION*, 1958

Jack Gould, n. d.

Almost everyone I knew in New York had first arrived there in a fairly adult state instead of being born there. We had all reached that city because of legends as old as Horatio Alger. We had all come there to make good and to set the world on fire, and we had all been in a highly impressionable state.
JOHN P. MARQUAND, *MELVILLE GOODWIN, USA,* 1951

Joe Steinmetz, 1952

Its [suburbia's] clear indifference to the metropolitan world about it, and on which it clearly depends.

ROBERT C. WOOD, *SUBURBIA: ITS PEOPLE AND THEIR POLITICS,* **1959**

Jack Gould, n. d.

Jack Gould, 1954

Jack Gould, 1954

The automobile has made it easy to move away and leave our problems behind. Instead of clearing out the slums, people have been clearing out for the suburbs. . . . But escape from the central city to the fringes has turned out to be no escape at all. . . . The natural beauty of the countryside is being thrown to the bulldozers.

WILFRED OWEN, *CITIES IN THE MOTOR AGE,* 1959

53

Time spent going to and from work, time spent in hauling children, time spent in class, the weekend for work, the weekend for "career maneuvering" or "improving" social status, all are by the clock. . . . Endlessly active, constantly harassed, the suburbanite hurries everywhere, caught up in a chain of events never of his own making but from which he cannot withdraw. He is plunged into a "hotbed of participation," an endless circle of meetings, appointments, arrivals, departures, and consultations.
ROBERT C. WOOD, *SUBURBIA: ITS PEOPLE AND THEIR POLITICS*, 1959

The children themselves, in fact, before they get access to a car, are captives of their suburb. . . . In the suburban public schools, the young are captives too, dependent on whatever art and science and general liveliness their particular school happens to have.
DAVID RIESMAN, "THE SUBURBAN DISLOCATION," IN *ABUNDANCE FOR WHAT? AND OTHER ESSAYS*, 1957

Typical American behavior is to solve a problem of transit congestion by creating a parallel system that builds up new neighborhoods and redoubles the transit congestion.
PERCIVAL GOODMAN AND PAUL GOODMAN, *COMMUNITAS: MEANS OF LIVELIHOOD AND WAYS OF LIFE*, 1947

A development [in the suburbs] is essentially an homogeneous matriarchy, and it does not matter whether it is an homogeneous matriarchy of veterans' families or an homogeneous matriarchy of Texas oil billionaires or an homogeneous matriarchy of New York Divorcees. The simple fact is, look-alike people act alike in look-alike homes.
JOHN KEATS, *THE CRACK IN THE PICTURE WINDOW*, 1956

Certainly the drive for high-value and only high-value property buttresses the social and ethnic exclusiveness which suburbanites display in their search for small town homogeneity. . . . [T]o be liberal in their attitude toward lower-income newcomers, to strive for heterogeneous neighborhoods, to welcome citizens regardless of race, creed, or color . . . is to invite financial disaster.
ROBERT C. WOOD, *SUBURBIA: ITS PEOPLE AND THEIR POLITICS*, 1959

Jack Rodden, 1951

I keep picturing all these little kids playing some game in this big field of rye. . . . Thousands of little kids, and nobody's around—nobody big, I mean . . . except me. And I'm standing on the edge of some crazy cliff. . . . I'd just be the catcher in the rye.

J. D. SALINGER, *CATCHER IN THE RYE*, 1951

Joe Steinmetz, 1954

Joe Steinmetz, 1957

Legler, c. 1946

Jack Gould, n. d.

Perhaps the best thing about our farmhouse was that it had a large old-fashioned kitchen, with a pantry that served as a secondary workroom for messier jobs. . . . [T]he main thing about it was that it was spacious and many activities besides cooking went on there; for here is where the loot of Geddes's trapping and hunting would be piled; here is where . . . he might . . . play dominoes or chess with John; here is where he tested his traps, wound his fishing lines, greased his boots, or just lounged about and chatted with his mother. . . . [T]he kitchen was the great common family domain, and it could not have served its purposes if it had been planned for cooking alone. Mark that, you economical architects and you close calculators of costs per square foot!

LEWIS MUMFORD, "THE KITCHEN—WHAT WENT ON THERE," IN *GREEN MEMORIES*, **1947**

Harry Annas, 1952

Regional differences in taste have all but disappeared, and if you were to be put down blindfolded in the new suburbs of any large American city it would be difficult to tell if you were in the East or the West, the North or the South. Sears Roebuck and Company, the largest retailer in the world, have given up the custom of printing different catalogues for different parts of the country; the same sofa covered in the same material sells at almost precisely the same rate in each of six sales districts into which they divide the country. The same is true of lamps, and pictures for the wall, and women's dresses.

RUSSELL LYNES, *THE TASTEMAKERS*, 1949

Robert Burian, 1948

If we were the kind to follow the Pattern, I'll tell you just what we would do. First, in a couple of years, we'd move out to Ferncrest Village (it's really pretty tacky there, you know). We wouldn't go straight to Eastmere Hills—that would look pushy at this stage of the game. . . . About that time, we'd change from Christ Church to St. Edwards, and we'd start going to the Fortnightlys. . . . Then about ten years later, we'd finally build in Eastmere Hills.

WILLIAM H. WHYTE, JR., "THE WIVES OF MANAGEMENT," *FORTUNE* **OCTOBER 1951**

Lucien Brown, 1958

Joe Steinmetz, 1953

You might write: business manager, cook, nurse, chauffeur, dressmaker, interior decorator, accountant, caterer, teacher, private secretary—or just put down philanthropist.
DOROTHY THOMPSON, "OCCUPATION HOUSEWIFE," *LADIES' HOME JOURNAL* **MARCH 1949**

"Jo-Lea, Jo-Lea," he heard his voice in a painful grating sound, as the words were ripped out, "durn it, Jo-Lea, I just love you!"
ROBERT PENN WARREN, *THE CAVE*, 1959

They were together as much as their studies allowed, which is to say almost constantly, every week end and on Wednesdays and Thursdays and even Tuesdays, when Dick would make the long afternoon drive over the mountains to Sweet Briar. . . . [A]lone they allowed their arms to envelop each other, and threaded the hot clock of their desire with kisses and frank hoarse demands, which neither of them expected or really wanted, to be fulfilled.
WILLIAM STYRON, *LIE DOWN IN DARKNESS*, 1951

The most saddening thing is to admit that I am not in love. I can only love (if that means self-denial—or does it mean self-fulfillment? Or both?) by giving up my love, of self and ambitions.
SYLVIA PLATH, FROM HER JOURNALS WRITTEN WHILE AT SMITH COLLEGE, 1950-55

Joe Steinmetz, 1952

Jack Gould, 1946

Jack Gould, 1946

Joe Steinmetz, 1954

68

Harry Annas, n. d.

Martin Schweig, 1955

Martin Schweig, 1959

Increasingly, individuals seek escape from the freedom of impersonality, secularism, and individualism. They look for community in marriage, thus putting, often, an intolerable strain upon a tie already grown institutionally fragile.

ROBERT A. NISBET, *THE QUEST FOR COMMUNITY: A STUDY IN THE ETHICS OF ORDER AND FREEDOM,* 1953

John Deusing, n. d.

The expense account has become a way of life. There is not only travel, there are luncheon clubs, company retreats, special conventions, parties, and perquisites, and though the wife may be thrown an occasional convention as a crumb, the expense-account world rarely encompasses her. It is primarily a man's world. . . . [H]e is likely to find the pattern of life at 7118 Crestmere Road dull in comparison.

WILLIAM H. WHYTE, JR., "THE WIVES OF MANAGEMENT," *FORTUNE* **OCTOBER 1951**

Martin Schweig, 1955

During the last few years he had relied upon her steadfast gaze of love and longing, . . . which supported him against the unthinkable notion that life was not rich and purposeful and full of rewards. . . . She was submissive and she worshipped him, and it was for those reasons that he had loved her: . . . he talked and she listened, while through this curious interplay of self-esteem and self-effacement there ran an undercurrent of emotion they were both obliged to call love.

WILLIAM STYRON, *LIE DOWN IN DARKNESS*, **1951**

Jack Gould, 1952

Lucien Brown, n. d.

He had married a girl in a chiffon dress who had once fainted when a mouse ran over her shoe—
and mysteriously she had become a grey-haired housewife with a business of her own and even
some Coca-Cola stock. He lived now in a curious vacuum surrounded by the concerns of family life
. . . and the daily activities swirled around him as dead leaves ring the center of a whirlpool, leaving
him curiously untouched.

CARSON McCULLERS, *CLOCK WITHOUT HANDS*, 1953

My usual work week is seventy to eighty hours. . . . I get to the office at 8:30 A.M. and usually am at my desk until 6:00 P.M. . . . and three nights a week I take home a brief case with reading material and reports.
WILLIAM H. WHYTE, JR., *THE ORGANIZATION MAN*, 1956

[*H*]*ow* do the wives conceive their own role? . . . As they explain it, the good *wife* is good by *not* doing things—by *not* complaining when her husband works late; by *not* fussing when a transfer is coming up; by *not* engaging in any controversial activity. . . . [T]he bad wife, clearly, is one who obtrudes too much . . . or simply, someone who pushes her man around.
WILLIAM H. WHYTE, JR., "THE WIVES OF MANAGEMENT," *FORTUNE* OCTOBER 1951

The typical executives, today and in the past, were born with a big advantage: they managed to have fathers on at least upper middle-class levels of occupation and income; they are Protestant, white, and American-born. . . . They are well educated.
C. WRIGHT MILLS, *THE POWER ELITE*, 1956

Second nature to the seasoned wife . . . are the following:

Don't turn up at the office unless you absolutely have to.
Don't get too chummy with the wives of associates your husband might soon pass on the way up.
Be attractive. There is a strong correlation between executive success and the wife's appearance.
Never—repeat never—get tight at a company party (it may go down in a dossier).
WILLIAM H. WHYTE, JR., "THE WIVES OF MANAGEMENT," *FORTUNE* OCTOBER 1951

Management, therefore, has a challenge and an obligation to deliberately plan and create a favorable, constructive attitude on the part of the wife that will liberate her husband's total energies for the job.
WILLIAM H. WHYTE, JR., "THE WIVES OF MANAGEMENT," *FORTUNE* OCTOBER 1951

"I sort of look forward to the day my kids are grown up," one sales manager said. "Then I won't have to have such a guilty conscience about neglecting them."
WILLIAM H. WHYTE, JR., *THE ORGANIZATION MAN*, 1956

Frances Sullivan, 1955

Jean Raeburn, 1952

Joe Steinmetz, 1952

Do head work while dusting, sweeping, washing dishes, paring potatoes, etc. Plan family recreation, the garden, etc.

BETTY CROCKER'S PICTURE COOK BOOK, 1956

Ike runs the country, and I turn the pork chops. . . . I had a career. His name was Ike.

"MAMIE, AS MORE THAN A 1950'S WOMAN," *NEW YORK TIMES* 17 NOVEMBER 1996

Lucien Brown, n. d.

Household skills take her into the garment trades; neat and personable, she becomes office worker and saleslady; patient and dexterous, she does well on repetitive, detailed factory work; compassionate, she becomes teacher and nurse.

"THE AMERICAN WOMAN: HER ACHIEVEMENTS AND TROUBLES," *LIFE* 24 DECEMBER 1956

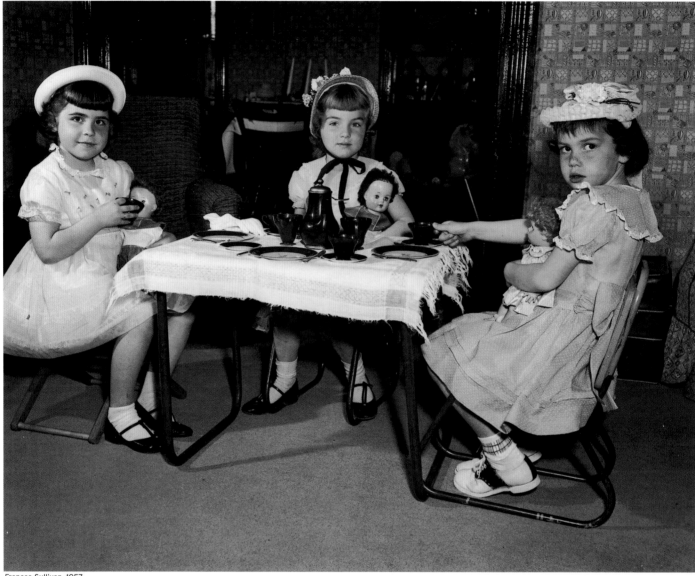

Frances Sullivan, 1957

Jack Gould, 1957

Martin Schweig, n. d.

It is not enough now that he work hard; he must be a damn good fellow to boot.

WILLIAM H. WHITE, JR., *THE ORGANIZATION MAN*, 1956

Now take the man who drives a Studebaker, smokes Old Golds, uses cream-based hair oil, an electric shaver, carries a Parker 51 fountain pen. Obviously he's a salesman, an active man, aggressive in face-to-face situations and wants to make a good impression.

VANCE PACKARD, *THE HIDDEN PERSUADERS*, 1957

Joe Steinmetz, 1954

The year, 1956, President and Mrs. Dwight D. Eisenhower mention as one of their favorites a dinner menu that almost any American citizen can enjoy in his own home.

Broiled Sirloin Steak
Baked Potatoes
Green Beans
Green Salad with French Dressing
Apple Pie with Cheese and Coffee

"AT THE WHITE HOUSE, WASHINGTON D.C.," *BETTY CROCKER'S PICTURE COOK BOOK,* 1956

Bachrach Studio, 1947

Lucien Brown, n. d.

The faces at the other tables had a definite conformity, in spite of differences in features. They all bore the imprint of similar experience. They were all assured.

JOHN P. MARQUAND, *MELVILLE GOODWIN, USA*, 1951

Bachrach Studio, 1959

"Dave and I have often thought about going back to East Wells," a successful young executive's wife explains. "It's a beautiful old New England town and we both had such happy times there. But all the people who had anything on the ball seem to have left. There are a few who took over their fathers' business[es], but the rest—I hate to sound so snobbish, but, dammit, I *do* feel superior to them. . . . a return carries overtones of failure."

WILLIAM H. WHYTE, JR., *THE ORGANIZATION MAN*, 1956

Jack Gould, 1951

All of this by no means excludes the fact that the father is potentially quite a man, but he shows it more away from home, in business, on camping trips, and in his club. As the son becomes aware of this, a new, almost astonished respect is added to his affection.

ERIK ERIKSON, *CHILDHOOD AND SOCIETY,* **1950**

Jack Gould, 1946

[T]he patient of today suffers most under the problem of what he should believe in and who he should . . . be or become, while the patient of early psychoanalysis suffered most under inhibitions which prevented him from being what and who he thought he knew he was.

ERIK ERIKSON, *CHILDHOOD AND SOCIETY*, 1950

The dominant direction of feminine training and development today . . . discourages just those traits necessary to the attainment of sexual pleasure: receptivity and passiveness . . . with a deep inward-ness and readiness for the final goal of sexual life—impregnation.

FERDINAND LUNDBERG AND MARYNIA FARNHAM, *MODERN WOMAN: THE LOST SEX*, 1947

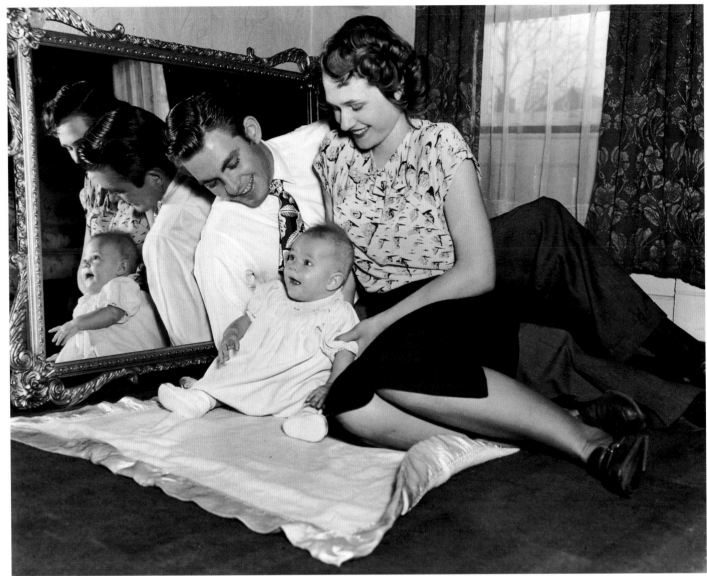

Martin Schweig, 1948

Caring for a baby is a full-time taxing job. It's a big change from 8-hour a day work you could leave behind you at night. . . . Don't be surprised if you feel depressed and let down when you first have the full care of your baby. . . . [I]t is a blow to find you get exhausted very easily and that your strength doesn't come back as fast as you supposed it would. . . . You'd lose confidence fast in any book that forgot to mention the kind of day when you're mopping up spilled orange-juice, while the baby's howling and the telephone's ringing—only three dry diapers left, . . . and a steady rain coming down outside. . . . To feel that you must let him dictate exactly when he must be fed leaves your needs completely out of account. . . . Your low spirits may be added to if your friends and relatives seem to have eyes and thoughts only for the baby.

INFANT CARE, CHILDREN'S BUREAU PUBLICATION NO. 8, 1951

Joe Steinmetz, n. d.

For his spirit to grow normally he needs someone to dote on him, to think he's the most wonderful baby in the world, to make noises and baby talk at him, to hug and smile at him, to keep him company during waking periods. . . . Every time you pick your baby up, . . . every time you change him, bathe him, feed him, smile at him, he's getting a feeling that he belongs to you and that you belong to him. Nobody else in the world, no matter how skilled, can give that to him. . . . [I]f anything needs to be done for thumbsucking it should be to make the child's life more satisfying.

BENJAMIN SPOCK, *BABY AND CHILD CARE,* **1946**

Babies control and bring up their families as much as they are controlled by them.

ERIK ERIKSON, *CHILDHOOD AND SOCIETY*, 1950

I'd like six kids. I don't know why I say that—it just seems like a minimum production goal.

DAVID RIESMAN, "THE FOUND GENERATION," *THE AMERICAN SCHOLAR* AUTUMN 1956

[I]n their uneasiness as to how to bring up children they turn increasingly to books, magazines, government pamphlets, and radio programs. . . . She learns that there are no problem children, only problem parents; and she learns to look into her own psyche whenever she is moved to deny the children anything, including an uninterrupted flow of affection. If the children are cross then the mother must be withholding something.

DAVID RIESMAN WITH NATHAN GLAZER AND REUEL DENNY, *THE LONELY CROWD: A STUDY OF THE CHANGING AMERICAN CHARACTER*, 1950

Lucien Brown, 1955

Lucien Brown, 1950

Lucien Brown, n. d.

But even if a child has thought he wanted a brother or sister, he won't enjoy being neglected in its favor.

INFANT CARE, CHILDREN'S BUREAU PUBLICATION NO. 8, 1951

Every father and mother trembles lest an offspring, in act or thought, should be different from his fellows, and the smallest display of uniqueness in a child becomes the signal for the application of drastic measures.

ROBERT LINDNER, *PRESCRIPTION FOR REBELLION*, 1952

The teacher explained to me [a mother] that he was doing fine on his lessons but that his social adjustment was not as good as it might be. He would pick just one or two friends to play with, and sometimes he was happy to remain by himself.

WILLIAM H. WHYTE, JR., *THE ORGANIZATION MAN*, 1956

BERNICE. Frankie, the whole idea of a club is that there are members who are included and the non-members who are not included. Now what you want to do is to round up a club of your own. And you could be the president yourself.

FRANKIE. Who would I get?

BERNICE. Why, those little children you hear playing in the neighborhood.

FRANKIE. I don't want to be president of all those little young left-over people.

CARSON McCULLERS, *THE MEMBER OF THE WEDDING*, 1946

[T]his was something worse than a physical hurt, and he was crying. He wouldn't go to school ever again on the day they had religious instruction. . . . He'd had to sit out in the hall by himself, and all the kids walking down the hall to get a drink or run an errand had thought he'd been put there as punishment and had teased him. He knew they'd tease him still more if he said he was there because he couldn't attend religious instruction classes, so he'd let them think he was there for being bad.

VASHTI CROMWELL McCOLLUM, *ONE WOMAN'S FIGHT*, 1951

The daily schedule is an effort, with mother as chauffeur and booking agent to cultivate all the currently essential talents, especially the gregarious ones. It is inconceivable to some supervising adults that a child might prefer his own company or that of just one other child.

DAVID RIESMAN WITH NATHAN GLAZER AND REUEL DENNEY, *THE LONELY CROWD: A STUDY OF THE CHANGING AMERICAN CHARACTER*, 1950

Lucien Brown, n. d.

Lucien Brown, 1953

America's most widely circulated book on the care of infants . . . makes the sweeping assertion that "it's a sensible rule not to take a child into the parents' bed for any reason." It seems clear beyond dispute that the household space provided by the economy of abundance has been used to emphasize the separateness, the apartness, if not the isolation, of the American child.

DAVID M. POTTER, *PEOPLE OF PLENTY: ECONOMIC ABUNDANCE AND THE AMERICAN CHARACTER,* **1954**

Jack Gould, n. d.

Will I be pretty?/Will I be rich?

FROM THE SONG "QUE SERA, SERA," BY JAY LIVINGSTON AND RAY EVANS, 1955

Jack Gould, 1947

Lucien Brown, n. d.

Jack Gould, 1950

Lucien Brown, 1953

Lucien Brown, n. d.

Lucien Brown, 1953

Lucien Brown, n. d.

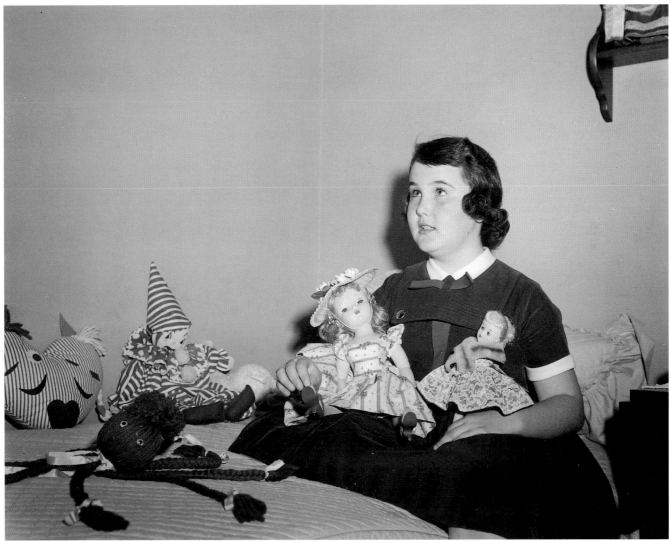

Lucien Brown, n. d.

Frances Sullivan, 1956

Lucien Brown, n. d.

Deusing Studio, 1947

A great many children have unquestionably been damaged psychologically by the spinster teacher, who cannot be an adequate model of a complete woman.

FERDINAND LUNDBERG AND MARYNIA F. FARNHAM, M.D., *MODERN WOMAN: THE LOST SEX*, 1947

Frances Sullivan, 1958

Today, youth has abandoned solitude, it has relinquished privacy; instead, these are the days of pack-running.

ROBERT LINDNER, *MUST YOU CONFORM?*, **1956**

Jack Gould, n. d.

Lucien Brown, n. d.

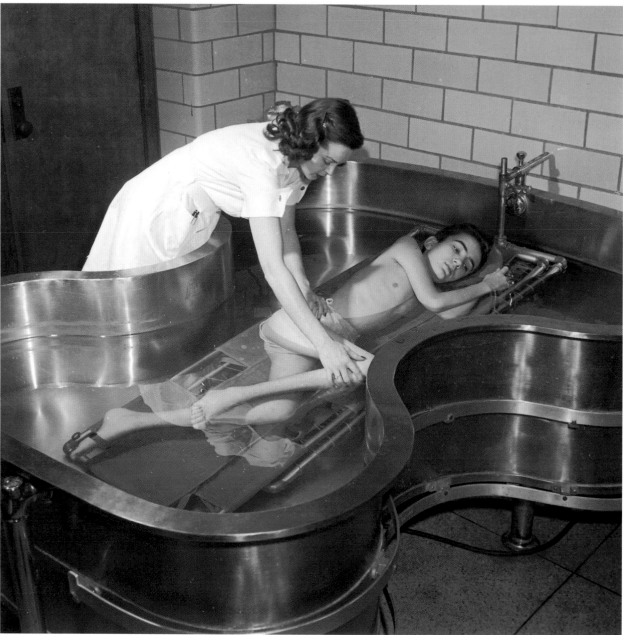

Jack Gould, 1947

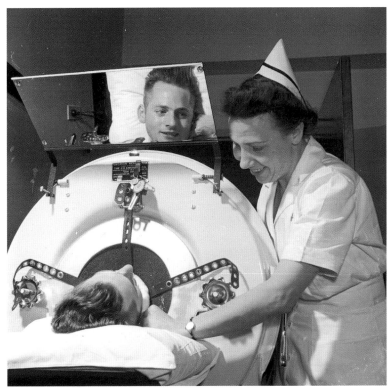

Jack Gould, 1947

Jack Gould, 1947

Jack Gould, 1948

Jack Gould, 1948

Jack Gould, 1953

Joe Steinmetz, n. d.

[W]e refer to adolescents today as teen-agers rather than simply as "youth": the latter term has a futuristic ring, implying that youth will do things and change things, while the term "teen-ager" . . . has a highly self-conscious but also patronizing quality, referring as it does to a kind of protected or encapsulated and not quite real life.

DAVID RIESMAN, "THE STUDY OF NATIONAL CHARACTER: SOME OBSERVATIONS ON THE AMERICAN CASE," *THE HARVARD LIBRARY BULLETIN* **XIII, NO. 1, 1959**

Jack Gould, 1952

A. I like Superman better than the others because they can't do everything Superman can do. Batman can't fly and that is very important.

Q. Would you like to be able to fly?

A. I would like to be able to fly if everybody else did, but otherwise it would be kind of conspicuous."

KATHERINE M. WOLFE AND MARJORIE FISKE, "THE CHILDREN TALK ABOUT COMICS," *COMMUNICATIONS RESEARCH 1948-1949*, **EDS. PAUL F. LAZARSFELD AND FRANK STANTON, 1949**

Gene Claseman, 1955

Jack Gould, 1950

Gene Claseman, 1958

God, who am I? . . . And I sit here without identity: faceless. My head aches. There is history to read . . . centuries to comprehend before I sleep, millions of lives to assimilate before breakfast tomorrow.

SYLVIA PLATH, FROM HER JOURNALS WRITTEN WHILE AT SMITH COLLEGE, 1950-55

Jack Gould, n. d.

Nowadays the sense of self is deficient. The questions of adolescence — "Who am I?" "Where am I going?" "What is the meaning of life?" . . . receive no final answers.

ALLEN WHEELIS, *THE QUEST FOR IDENTITY*, 1958

Jack Gould, n. d.

More than that: (I) the media tell the man in the mass who he is—they give him identity; (2) they tell him what he wants to be—they give him aspirations; (3) they tell him how to get that way—they give him technique; and (4) they tell him how to feel that he is that way even when he is not—they give him escape.
C. WRIGHT MILLS, *THE POWER ELITE*, 1956

The cosmetic manufacturers are not selling lanolin, they are selling hope. . . .
We no longer buy oranges, we buy vitality. We do not buy just an auto, we buy prestige.
VANCE PACKARD, *THE HIDDEN PERSUADERS*, 1957

Most of "the pictures in our heads" we have gained from these media.
C. WRIGHT MILLS, *THE POWER ELITE*, 1956

In the focus of public attention the old captains of industry have been replaced by an entirely new type: the "Captains of Nonindustry, of Consumption and Leisure."
DAVID RIESMAN WITH NATHAN GLAZER AND REUEL DENNY, *THE LONELY CROWD: A STUDY OF THE CHANGING AMERICAN CHARACTER*, 1950

At one of the largest advertising agencies in America psychologists . . . are probing sample humans in an attempt to find how to identify, and beam messages to people of high anxiety, body con-sciousness, hostility, passiveness, and so on.
VANCE PACKARD, *THE HIDDEN PERSUADERS*, 1957

Jack Gould, 1948

Martin Schweig, n. d.

The time is past when a boy's chief possession was his bike and a girl's party wardrobe consisted of a fancy dress worn with a string of dime-store pearls. What Depression-bred parents may think of as luxuries are looked on as necessities by their offspring.

"A NEW $10 BILLION POWER: THE U.S. TEEN-AGE CONSUMER," *LIFE* 31 AUGUST 1959

Joe Steinmetz, n. d.

All history can show no more portentous economic phenomena than today's American market. It is colossal, soaking up half the world's steel and oil, and three-fourths of its cars and appliances.
FORTUNE AUGUST 1953

Jack Gould, 1952

Harry Annas, 1946

One ad executive explained with fervor: "What makes this country great is the creation of wants and desires."

VANCE PACKARD, *THE HIDDEN PERSUADERS,* **1957**

[T]he amount spent for advertising in the United States in 1951 was $6,548,000,000. . . . [T]he amount is equivalent to $199 per year for every separate family in the United States. Compare this with what the nation paid for primary and secondary public education in 1949, which amounted to a total expenditure of $5,010,000,000. This means that for every household, we paid $152. . . . [E]veryone knows that we have, per capita, more automobiles, more telephones, more radios, more vacuum cleaners, more electric lights, more bathtubs, more supermarkets and movie palaces and hospitals, than any other nation. . . . [T]he factor of relative abundance is, by general consent, a basic condition of American life.

DAVID M. POTTER, *PEOPLE OF PLENTY: ECONOMIC ABUNDANCE AND THE AMERICAN CHARACTER*, 1954

I drew housewives, who, until they reached for the right soap flakes, laid themselves wide open to straggly hair, poor posture, unruly children, disaffected husbands, rough (but slender) hands, untidy (but enormous) kitchens.

J. D. SALINGER, *NINE STORIES*, 1953

Material improvement that is unaccompanied by a sense of personal belonging may actually intensify social dislocation and personal frustration.

ROBERT A. NISBET, *THE QUEST FOR COMMUNITY: A STUDY IN THE ETHICS OF ORDER AND FREEDOM*, 1953

Frances Sullivan, 1949

Joe Steinmetz, 1959

Jean Raeburn, 1950

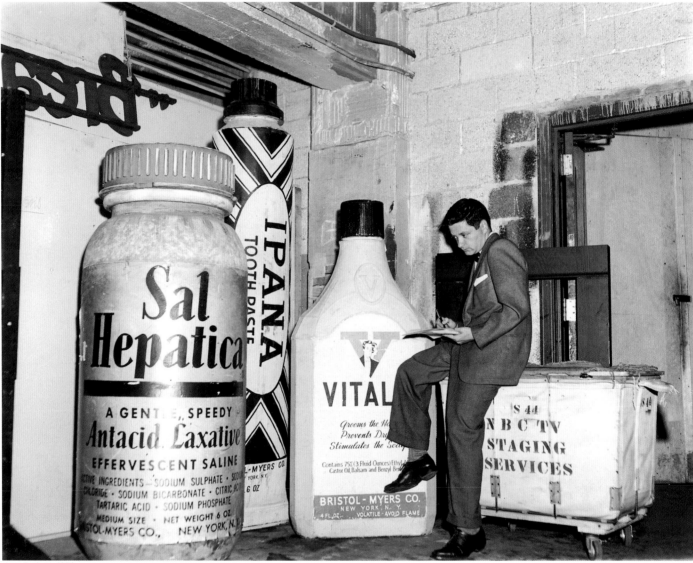

Jean Raeburn, 1950

Jack Gould, 1948

Mr. But is the man who is broad-minded—sensible, practical, and proud of his Christianity. Listen to the great American, Mr. But:

"Now nobody can say that I'm not a friend of the Mexicans or that I am prejudiced, BUT—"

"Nobody can say that I am anti-Semitic. Why some of my best friends are Jews, BUT—"

"Surely nobody can think of me as a reactionary, BUT—"

"I don't think anyone in this room feels more sympathetic toward the Negroes than I do. I've always had a number of them working for me, BUT—"

SAUL D. ALINSKY, *REVEILLE FOR RADICALS*, 1946

First we registered for the vote in a body, and if you don't think that takes nerve in this country you don't know nothing. Each member got a little cardboard coffin with his name in it and a printed sign, "A voting reminder."

CARSON McCULLERS, *CLOCK WITHOUT HANDS*, 1953

He remembered the people he had seen in the city, whose eyes held no love for him. And he thought of their feet so swift and brutal, and the dark grey clothes they wore, and how when they passed they did not see him, or if they saw him, they smirked.

JAMES BALDWIN, *GO TELL IT ON THE MOUNTAIN*, 1952-53

Sherman was convinced that all white Southerners were crazy. Lynching a Negro boy because a white woman said he had whistled at her. A Judge sentencing a Negro because a white woman said she didn't like the way he looked at her. Whistling! Looking! His prejudiced mind was inflamed and quivering like some tropical atmosphere that causes mirages.

CARSON McCULLERS, *CLOCK WITHOUT HANDS*, 1953

"Keep 'Bama white."

"Let's kill her! Kill her!"

"Hey, hey, ho, where in the hell did Autherine go? Hey, hey, ho, where in the hell did that nigger go?"

QUOTES FROM THE WHITE CROWD AGAINST AUTHERINE LUCY BECOMING THE FIRST BLACK STUDENT AT THE UNIVERSITY OF ALABAMA, TUSCALOOSA, 1956

"The reason they act so queer," Little Crane pointed out, "is because they're not an original people. Now we Indians are an original people. The Great Being made us from the beginning. Look! Our hair is always black, our eyes and skin dark, even True Son's here. But the whites are of colors like horses. Some are light, some are dark, some are in-between. Some have black hair; some have light hair. . . . Their eyes are fickle as their hair."

CONRAD RICHTER, *THE LIGHT IN THE FOREST*, 1953

Martin Schweig, 1955

Harry Annas, 1953

Robert Burian, 1946

Frances Sullivan, 1955

Joe Steinmetz, 1950

It is the peculiar triumph of society—and its loss—that it is able to convince those people to whom it has given inferior status of the reality of this decree; it has the force and the weapons to translate its dictum into fact, so that the allegedly inferior are actually made so, insofar as the societal realities are concerned.

JAMES BALDWIN, *NOTES OF A NATIVE SON*, 1955

134

Jack Gould, n. d.

Joe Steinmetz, n. d.

C. Bennette Moore, n. d.

Aunt Jemima and Uncle Tom are dead, their places taken by a group of amazingly well-adjusted young men and women, almost as dark, but ferociously literate, well-dressed and scrubbed, who are never laughed at, who are not likely ever to set foot in a cotton or tobacco field or in any but the most modern of kitchens. . . . Before, however, our joy at the demise of Aunt Jemima and Uncle Tom approaches the indecent, we had better ask whence they sprang, how they lived? Into what limbo have they vanished?

JAMES BALDWIN, *GO TELL IT ON THE MOUNTAIN,* **1952-53**

Sam Cooper, 1956

Joe Steinmetz, 1958

Martin Schweig, 1951

Joe Steinmetz, c. 1950

Jack Gould, n. d.

George Durette, 1946

[Nineteen fifty-two] first found admen in the very highest policy-making councils of both parties: for the first time, candidates became "merchandise," political campaigns were "sales promotion jobs," the electorate was a "market."

JOHN G. SCHNEIDER, *THE GOLDEN KAZOO*, 1956

Joe Steinmetz, 1946

Jack Gould, 1950

To avoid destruction the United States need only measure up to its own best traditions and prove itself worthy of preservation as a great nation.
GEORGE F. KENNAN, "THE SOURCES OF SOVIET CONDUCT," *FOREIGN AFFAIRS* JULY 1947

Today—August 1, 1951—the Nylon War enters upon the third month since the United States began all-out bombing of the Soviet Union with consumer's goods . . . [and] that if allowed to sample the riches of America, the Russian people would not long tolerate masters who gave them tanks and spies instead of vacuum cleaners and beauty parlors.
DAVID RIESMAN, "THE NYLON WAR," *INDIVIDUALISM RECONSIDERED*, 1954 (WRITTEN IN 1951)

But a large number of agreements were reached in spite of the setup—only to be broken as soon as the unconscionable Russian Dictator [Stalin] returned to Moscow! And I even liked the little son of a bitch.
HARRY TRUMAN, UNSENT LETTER TO DEAN ACHESON, 15 MARCH 1957

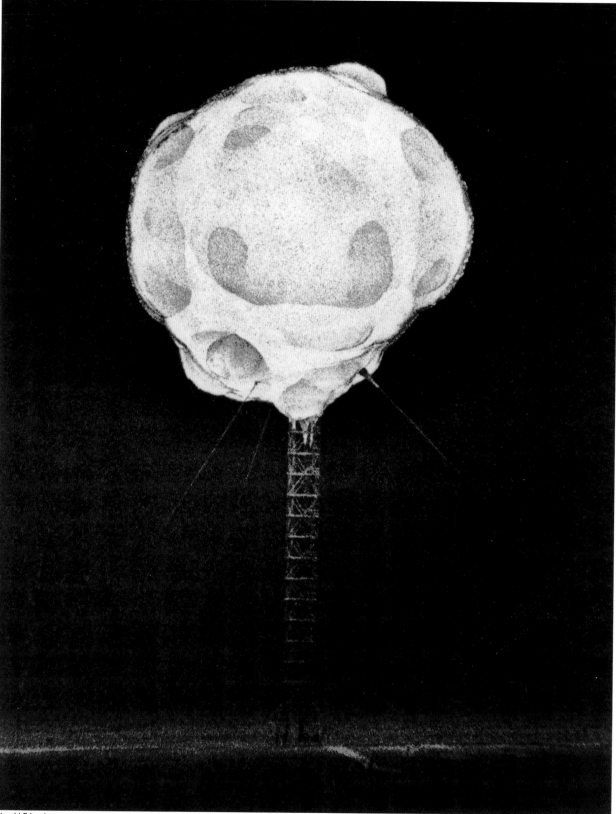

Harold Edgerton
Atomic Bomb

147

Jack Gould, n. d.

Lucien Brown, n. d.

But the radioactivity of the river plankton was 2,000 times higher, that of the ducks eating the plankton 40,000 times higher, that of the fish 150,000 times higher. In young swallows fed on insects caught by their parents in the river, the radioactivity was 500,000 times higher, and in the egg yolks of water birds more than 1,000,000 times higher. . . . To fail to consider its importance and its consequences would be a folly for which humanity would have to pay a terrible price.

ALBERT SCHWEITZER'S STATEMENT TO THE ATOMIC ENERGY COMMISSION, 23 APRIL 1957

Mr. Dean asked whether it was considered necessary to make a public announcement concerning the unusually high yield of the device to be tested. Mr. Graves and General Fields said that they considered it unnecessary to go beyond the information contained in the draft press release.

ATOMIC ENERGY COMMISSION MEETING #863, 18 MAY 1953

At times some of you have been exposed to potential risk from flash, blast, or fallout. You have accepted the inconvenience or the risk without fuss, without alarm, and without panic. . . . [E]ach shot is justified by national and international security need.

"A MESSAGE TO PEOPLE WHO LIVE NEAR NEVADA TEST SITE," FROM THE ATOMIC ENERGY COMMISSION BOOKLET *ATOMIC TEST EFFECTS IN THE NEVADA TEST SITE REGION*, **JANUARY 1955**

People feel—and they are bang right—that there is not much point in initiating large-scale and long-range improvements in the physical environment, when we are uncertain about the existence of a physical environment the day after tomorrow.

PERCIVAL GOODMAN AND PAUL GOODMAN, *COMMUNITAS: MEANS OF LIVELIHOOD AND WAYS OF LIFE*, **1947**

This mysterious heavenly visitor [Halley's comet] is due again in 1985, at which time there is every likelihood the earth will be completely destroyed, I hope. This is not as bad as it would have been in 1910, because in 1985 only turtle life will be left on the planet because of the atom bomb.

JAMES THURBER, FROM A LETTER WRITTEN IN 1946

[T]he State Department . . . is thoroughly infested with Communists. . . . I have in my hand 57 cases of individuals who would appear to be either card-carrying members or certainly loyal to the Communist Party.

SENATOR JOSEPH McCARTHY, U.S. CONGRESS, *SENATE CONGRESSIONAL RECORD*, 81ST CONG., 2D SESS. 1950

[I]n spite of the fear which haunts the nation and breeds such bigotry, persecution, and injustice[,] I maintain the very unpopular position of opposing the present internal destruction of the democratic ideals by those fear-ridden fools who see communism everywhere.

SAUL ALINSKY, LETTER WRITTEN TO JACQUES MARITAIN, 20 FEBRUARY 1951

BETTY. I saw George Jacobs with the Devil! I saw Goody Howe with the Devil!

PARRIS. She speaks! She speaks!

BETTY. I saw Martha Bellows with the Devil!

ABIGAIL. I saw Goody Sibber with the Devil!

PUTNAM. The marshal, I'll call the marshal!

BETTY. I saw Alice Barrow with the Devil!

HALE. Let the marshal bring irons!

ABIGAIL. I saw Goody Hawkins with the Devil!

ARTHUR MILLER, *THE CRUCIBLE*, 1952

I think the most alarming spectacle today is not the spectacle of the atomic bomb in an unfederated world, it is the spectacle of Americans beginning to accept the device of loyalty oaths and witch-hunts, beginning to call anyone they don't like a Communist.

E. B. WHITE'S LETTER TO JANICE WHITE, 1952

[I]t is generally believed that those who engage in overt acts of perversion lack the emotional stability of normal persons. In addition there is an abundance of evidence to sustain the conclusion that indulgence in acts of sex perversion weakens the moral fiber of an individual to a degree that he is not suitable for a position of responsibility.

"EMPLOYMENT OF HOMOSEXUALS AND OTHER SEX PERVERTS IN GOVERNMENT," INTERIM REPORT SUBMITTED TO THE COMMITTEE ON EXPENDITURES IN EXECUTIVE DEPARTMENTS, U.S. SENATE, 81ST CONG., 1950

Let us not assassinate this lad further, Senator. You have done enough. Have you no sense of decency, sir, at long last?

JOSEPH WELCH, LAWYER FOR THE U.S. ARMY, TO SENATOR McCARTHY, U.S. CONGRESSIONAL SENATE SPECIAL SUBCOMMITTEE ON INVESTIGATION OF COMMITTEE ON GOVERNMENT OPERATIONS SPECIAL INVESTIGATION, 83D CONG., 2D SESS. 1954

We have carefully and conscientiously reviewed each and every one of the loyalty files relative to the individuals charged by Senator McCarthy. In no instance was any one of them now employed in the State Department found to be a "card-carrying Communist," a member of the Communist Party, or "loyal to the Communist Party."

U.S. CONGRESS, SENATE COMMITTEE ON FOREIGN RELATIONS, STATE DEPARTMENT EMPLOYEE LOYALTY INVESTIGATION, REPORT #2108, 81ST CONG., 2D SESS. 1950

Jack Gould, n. d.

Joe Steinmetz, n. d.

Jean Raeburn, 1952

[O]ne feature of these hierarchies of corporation, state, and military establishment is that their top positions are increasingly interchangeable. One result of this is the accumulative nature of prestige. Claims for prestige for example, may be initially based on military roles, then expressed in and augmented by an educational institution run by corporate executives, and cashed in, finally in the political order. . . . [H]igh military men have become accepted by other members of the political and economic elite, as well by broad sectors of the public, as authorities on issues that go well beyond what has historically been considered the proper domain of the military. . . . And in business circles the word has gone out: Get yourself a general.

C. WRIGHT MILLS, *THE POWER ELITE*, 1956

Joe Steinmetz, 1946

Time Line *

1945 V-E Day celebrates the formal end of the war in Europe. The Pottsdam Conference divides Germany into American, British, Russian, and French zones. MacArthur is named Allied Supreme Commander to accept Japanese surrender. Ho Chi Minh proclaims Vietnam an independent democratic republic. American and Russian troops occupy Korea. MacArthur accepts the surrender of the Japanese on the battleship *Missouri* in Tokyo Bay. The International Military Tribunal at Nuremburg tries twenty-four principal Nazi offenders. France elects Charles de Gaulle president. Josip Broz Tito's National Front secures a majority in the Yugoslavian election. Josef Kramer, the "Butcher of Belsen," is sentenced to death. The Senate approves U.S. participation in the United Nations. The United States recognizes Tito. Vitamin A is synthesized. The Nobel Prize in medicine goes to Alexander Fleming for the discovery of penicillin. "Bebop" is the new music. Weather radar is developed. The rationing of shoes, butter, and tires ends.

1946 The first session of the UN General Assembly begins in London. The UN General Assembly creates the UN Atomic Energy Commission to study the international control of atomic energy (but this plan is never realized because the Soviets wanted the United States to destroy all its atomic weapons). Sir Winston Churchill, in a speech at Fulton, Missouri, states that "from Stettin in the Baltic to Trieste in the Adriatic, an Iron Curtain has descended across the Continent." A loyalty program (established by Executive Order 9835) requires the investigation of all government employees and all applicants for government jobs. The war crimes trial begins in Tokyo. The Paris Peace Conference begins (and later breaks down). The United Mine Workers strike of 400,000 bituminous coal miners begins; Truman seizes the mines. The House Un-American Activities Committee holds closed hearings to investigate communist subversion in films. The Philippines wins independence from the United States. The U.S.

Supreme Court, in *Morgan v. Virginia,* finds that segregation on buses is unconstitutional. The United States tests an atomic bomb in Bikini atoll. Ho Chi Minh walks out of a conference on Indochina held in France. The U. S. creates the Bureau of Land Management. The American Indian Claims Commission is set up to deal with compensation for the Native Americans' loss of land. Secretary of Commerce Henry A. Wallace resigns after criticizing tough U. S. policy on the Soviet Union. The Nuremberg trials hang ten people for war crimes. French troops bombard Vietnam, killing 20,000. The Council of Foreign Ministers completes peace treaties with minor Axis nations. The newly formed United Nations chooses New York City as the site for its headquarters. The Fulbright Scholarships support study abroad. The United States loses 116 million worker days to strikes in the steel, automobile, coal, electrical equipment, and meat industries. The postwar baby boom begins in the United States with 3.4 million births. The Soviets take control of Eastern Europe. The United States produces 6,476 TV sets. Dr. Benjamin Spock publishes *The Common Sense Book of Baby and Child Care.* North Vietnam erupts in large-scale hostilities.

1947 The United States creates the Atomic Energy Commission. The first Dead Sea Scroll is found. Dr. Edwin Land demonstrates the Polaroid Land camera. The United States fires approximately 800 federal employees on "disloyalty charges." The House Committee on Un-American Activities begins hearings to restrict communist activities. The Centralia coal mine disaster highlights corruption in the supervision of the mines. The first offshore drilling rig is set up in the Gulf of Mexico. The draft ends. The Senate approves the Truman Doctrine. Rationing ends with the closing of the Office of Price Administration. William Libby discovers radiocarbon as a means of dating materials. The Japanese program of democratic reform approves their new constitution written by General Douglas MacArthur. In a speech at Harvard University, Secretary of State George Marshall presents the Marshall Plan to bolster the sagging European economy. Congress passes the Taft-Hartley Labor-Management Relations Act forbidding the closed shop. The first flying saucers allegedly fly over the Cascade Range and are labeled UFOs. Congress passes the National Security Act, which appoints secretaries to the army, navy, and air force and creates the CIA. The United States creates the Housing and Home Finance Agency. Congress passes the Foreign Assistance Act (the Marshall Plan). Great Britain gives India its independence. The World Series is on TV. William Levitt is the first to use an assembly-line system to build 2,000 identical houses on Long Island. President Truman televises the first broadcast from the White House. Chuck Yeager breaks the sound barrier. The UN General Assembly approves the division of Palestine into Arab and Jewish states. Raytheon introduces the microwave oven. The farming population drops to 19.3 percent of the total United States population. A dead moth in Mark II (the first programmable computer) leads to erroneous information, and the term *bug* is coined. U.S. college enrollment is 2.5 million, and over 1 million veterans attend under the GI Bill of Rights. The "Hollywood 10," members of the Screen Actors Guild, refuse to answer questions before the House Un-American Activities Committee and end up in prison. The United States produces 178,571 TV sets (each network produces between twenty-five and thirty hours of live programming a week). Joe DiMaggio (Yankees) is player of the year; rookie of the year is Jackie Robinson (Dodgers), the first African American in the majors. A newcomer to the Senate is Joseph McCarthy. Richard Nixon and Jack Kennedy are elected to the House.

1948 Mohandas Gandhi is assassinated. Orville Wright dies. Alfred Kinsey et al. publishes *Sexual Behavior in the Human Male.* A coup d'etat gives the communists control of the Czechoslovakian government. The first guided rocket is launched. The Supreme Court decides that teaching religion in public schools is unconstitutional. A new Ford sedan sells for $1,236 and a Chevy convertible for $1,750. The highest hourly wage rate in the United States (construction) is $2 an hour. The United Nations establishes the World Health Organization. Israel proclaims its independence. Arab nations invade Israel. The United States recognizes the new state of Israel. The Atomic Energy Commission announces the completion of three atomic tests at Eniwetok atoll. Moscow blocks access to Berlin after the United States, Britain, and France consolidate their separate occupation zones. The United States begins the Berlin airlift. The Selective Service Act registers all men between eighteen and twenty-five years of age but restricts induction to those between nineteen and twenty-five. The first elevator with electronic controls is installed. Production of long-playing records begins. The United States passes the first major Water Pollution Control Act. Truman acts to eliminate segregation in the armed services. Aureomycin chlortetracycline, the first broad-spectrum antibiotic, is discovered. Babe Ruth dies. Whittaker Chambers accuses Alger Hiss of being a member of the Communist Party. The *Chicago Daily Tribune* prints "Dewey Defeats Truman" headline; Truman is elected. Newcomers to the Senate are Hubert Humphrey and Lyndon Baines Johnson. The first McDonald's opens, offering fifteen-cent hamburgers, five-cent coffee, and ten-cent soft drinks. The record industry introduces 45-RPM records. The Cadillac company adds rounded tail fins, inspired by the Lockheed P-38 fighter, to its automobiles.

The first camera with interchangeable lenses and reflex focusing is marketed. Land Rover, the first four-wheel drive civilian car is produced. The first nonstop commercial flight across the Atlantic is made. Norbert Weiner publishes the first important study of computers, *Cybernetics.*

1949 Truman becomes president. Chiang Kai-shek gives up his command and takes Chinese Nationalists to Formosa. Truman introduces the first major civil rights bill since reconstruction. The first photograph of a gene is made. Arabs unite against Israel after Israel is given 21 percent more land than originally allotted. The National Cancer Institute links the rise in lung cancer to cigarette smoking. Twelve nations sign the North Atlantic Treaty Organization agreement stating that an attack on any one of them is an attack on all. Konrad Adenauer becomes the first chancellor of the new West German state. The Viking rocket is launched. The House passes the Central Intelligence Act, which exempts the CIA from audits and civil service regulations. The Russians explode their first atomic bomb. The communists establish the People's Republic in China, with Mao Tse-tung in power. The minimum wage increases from forty cents to seventy-five cents. The first long distance dial telephone is available. George Orwell writes *Nineteen Eighty-Four.* A urine test for pregnancy is made available. Ted Williams (Red Sox) is the player of the year in baseball.

1950 Ho Chi Minh's Democratic Republic of Vietnam is recognized by Peking and Moscow. The United States breaks with the People's Republic of China. Alger Hiss is convicted of perjury. The United States undertakes the development of the hydrogen bomb. The United States recognizes the Bao Dai's Saigon regime. The United States launches the first air-to-air rocket. Senator Joseph McCarthy charges that 205 communists are working in the State Department. The FBI issues the first Ten Most Wanted Criminals list. The United

States announces it will provide economic and military aid to the French in Indochina. North Korea invades South Korea, and the UN Security Council imposes military sanctions for the first time. The United States sends troops to South Korea. Senator Joseph McCarthy's charge of large-scale communist infiltration of the State Department is found to be untrue. The Atomic Energy Commission and the Department of Defense announce that low-burst atomic explosions do not represent a real danger to human beings. The McCarran Act (Internal Security Act) registers all communists. China forces Tibet to accept communist control. The nuclear test program moves to the Nevada Test Site.

1951 The Nevada Test Site holds the first aboveground atomic tests, and radiation increases across the country. The first general-purpose electronic computer for commercial sale is manufactured. Ethel and Julius Rosenberg are found guilty of selling atomic secrets to Russia. President Harry Truman fires Douglas MacArthur. Rocky Marciano knocks out Joe Louis. Joe DiMaggio retires. Troops are deliberately exposed to an atomic test and fallout to show they are safe. The first underground nuclear test is held at the Nevada Test Site.

1952 The twenty-second constitutional amendment, which limits the presidency to two terms, is passed. Dr. Jonas Salk produces the polio vaccine. The United States has the worst polio epidemic in its history with 57,244 cases. Nixon makes his Checkers speech on TV. The first successful open heart surgery is performed. The first Cinerama (wide screen) movie is made. John Kennedy is a new member of Congress. The United States creates the National Security Agency, which is free from congressional review.

1953 Dwight D. Eisenhower becomes president and Richard M. Nixon becomes vice president. Senator Joseph McCarthy becomes chair of the Senate Permanent Investigating Subcommittee of the Government Operations Committee. Joseph Stalin dies. The United States creates the Department of Health, Education, and Welfare. Francis Crick and James Watson announce the double-helix structure of DNA. Edmund Hillary and Tenzing Norgay are the first men to reach the summit of Mt. Everest. The United States executes the Rosenbergs in Sing Sing prison for atomic espionage. J. Robert Oppenheimer, former director of the Los Alamos Laboratory, is banned from access to classified material. The North Koreans sign an armistice. John F. Kennedy marries Jacqueline Lee Bouvier.

1954 The United States, using the Salk vaccine, administers the first mass polio immunization shots. The hydrogen bomb is exploded in the Marshall Islands. The Army-McCarthy hearings begin. The first successful insemination of women with stored frozen semen is achieved. The French surrender at Dien Bien Phu. In *Brown v. Board of Education of Topeka,* the Supreme Court unanimously holds that public school segregation is unconstitutional under the fourteenth amendment. There is convincing evidence that lung cancer occurs in smokers. The Geneva Accords partition Vietnam into the State of Vietnam in the North under Ho Chi Minh and the State of Vietnam in the South under Ngo Dinh Diem. The first commercial computer is put into operation at Princeton University. President Eisenhower signs a bill outlawing the Communist Party. The United Nations formally withdraws from Korea. The Southeast Asia Defense Treaty is formed to contain communism. Ellis Island is closed. The U.S. Senate votes to condemn McCarthy; after five years of accusations, he failed to uncover one communist. For the first time, the United States records more than 4 million births in one year.

The IBM 650 becomes the first mass-produced computer. The first successful kidney transplantation from a live donor is performed. The word *hell* is used for the first time in a movie, *On the Waterfront.* Elvis Presley debuts as a new recording artist.

1955 Albert Einstein dies. A presidential press conference is filmed for the first time. The United States takes over command of the South Vietnamese Army from France. James Dean dies in an automobile accident. Churchill, at age eighty, resigns as prime minister. West Germany becomes a sovereign state and joins NATO. The USSR signs the Warsaw Pact with Poland, Czechoslovakia, Hungary, Bulgaria, Romania, Albania, and East Germany. The Supreme Court rules that states must end racial segregation in public schools within a "reasonable" time. The first Disneyland opens south of Los Angeles. Two white men kidnap and kill Emmett Till, a fourteen-year-old African American boy alleged to have flirted with a white woman. Russia grants sovereignty to East Germany. Ngo Dinh Diem becomes president of Vietnam and declares South Vietnam an independent republic. The first use of transplants and plastic substitutes to restore normal blood flow to patients with hardened arteries. In Montgomery, Alabama, Rosa Parks refuses to give up her seat on a bus to a white man, and her action becomes the basis for a major civil rights action. Martin Luther King, Jr. leads a bus boycott. The AFL and CIO merge, and George Meany becomes president. Severo Ochoa synthesizes RNA. Yogi Berra (Yankees) is named player of the year in baseball.

1956 Autherine Lucy is the first African American to register at the University of Alabama; 1,000 rioters protest, the Board of Trustees forces her to withdraw "for her own safety," and eventually they expel her. All but three senators from the former Confederate States pledge to overturn the 1954 Supreme Court ruling on desegregation. The construction of the first U.S. 42,500-mile freeway system begins. The SS *Stockholm* rams into the *Andrea Doria* and the latter sinks. The use of fluoride reduces cavities by 60 percent. Russia invades Hungary. Israel invades the Sinai Peninsula and the Gaza Strip. The United Nations intervenes in the Suez Canal crisis. The first enclosed shopping center (mall) opens outside Minneapolis. In England, the first full-scale nuclear power station begins producing electricity. The first supersonic bomber (Convair B-58) is launched. The first fiber optics are invented. African Americans ride in the front of the bus in Montgomery, Alabama, for the first time. The first Kentucky Fried Chicken opens. Allen Ginsberg publishes *Howl, and Other Poems.* Mickey Mantle is player of the year in baseball.

1957 A group of African American ministers, including Martin Luther King, Jr., forms the Southern Christian Leadership Conference. The first electric wristwatch is marketed. IBM introduces FORTRAN. The Massachusetts Institute of Technology announces an inertial guidance system for missiles. Moscow announces the successful firing of the first long-range intercontinental ballistic missile; the United States responds by surrounding the USSR with nuclear missile bases. The national guard at Little Rock, Arkansas, blocks African American students from entering Central High School, but a federal injunction forces Governor Orval Faubus to remove the National Guard, and President Eisenhower sends federal troops to prevent "mob rule." A fire at Rocky Flats, Colorado, releases at least 1 million times the minimum permitted plutonium, but no warning is issued to

people living in the area. Eisenhower pledges to provide military and economic aid to any Middle Eastern country fighting communism (Eisenhower Doctrine). The Asian flu hits the United States. Strategic Air Command is placed on continuous alert. The first man-made satellite, *Sputnik,* is launched by Russia. *Sputnik II* takes the first living creature, a dog named Laika, into space; there is no recovery system. The United States appoints the first Civil Rights Commission to investigate infringement of minority rights. The United States launches the first successful Atlas rocket. The first atomic generator in the United States is built in Pennsylvania. Mickey Mantle is baseball's player of the year, and Ted Williams is the athlete of the year.

1958 A nuclear waste plant explodes in the Ural Mountains. Jimmy Hoffa takes over as president of the International Brotherhood of Teamsters. The communist paper, the *Daily Worker,* closes after thirty-four years. The Jupiter rocket takes the first U.S. satellite (*Explorer*) into orbit. The army tests the effect of LSD on unknowing soldiers. The first African American stewardess is hired by Mohawk Airlines. The United States experiences its first severe economic recession since World War II. The United States and Canada formalize the joint North American Air Defense Command. The United States creates the National Aeronautics and Space Administration. The first postal rate increase since 1932 raises the price of first-class letters from three to four cents per ounce. The Packard Motor Car Company stops production. Congress votes for the first presidential pensions ($25,000). Responding to world pressure and large fallout, the United States suspends nuclear tests for one year. France elects Charles de Gaulle as first president of the Fifth Republic. The John Birch Society is formed. We hear the first human voice from space via satellite. The first stereo long-playing records are marketed.

1959 Fidel Castro overthrows the dictatorship of Fulgencio Batista. Alaska becomes the forty-ninth state. The Dow Jones Industrial Average tops 600 for the first time. Scientists testify that a resumption of nuclear atmospheric testing will raise fallout levels beyond the danger point. NASA chooses the first astronauts, including John Glenn and Scott Carpenter. The first two Americans are killed in Vietnam as Hanoi takes control of the communist rebellion in South Vietnam, and North Vietnam attacks South Vietnamese troops for the first time. Governor Faubus submits to a federal ruling, and five African American students enroll in Little Rock, Arkansas, schools. Hawaii becomes the fiftieth state. *Explorer VI* transmits the first crude TV images of Earth. The first Barbie dolls appear on the market.

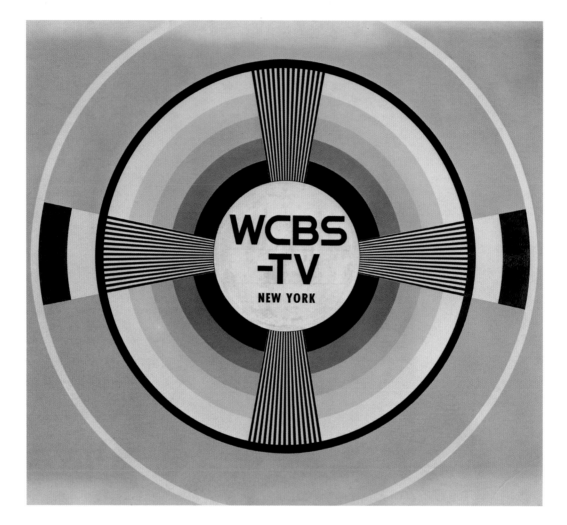

AIR-CONDITIONING, ANN LANDERS, ANTIBIOTICS, ANTIHISTAMINE DRUGS, ANTI-MISSILE MISSILE, ARMS RACE, ASTRONAU
BETTER DEAD THAN RED, BIKINI, BINAC, BIRTH CONTROL PILL, BRAINSTORMING, BRAINWASHING, BROADLOOM, BURGER
CINEMASCOPE, CLEAVAGE, COLD WAR, COMMIES, COMPUTER, CONSUMERISM, CONTAINMENT, CONTOUR SHEETS, COOKOUT, C
ABBY, DEEP FREEZE, DESEGREGATION, DISPOSABLE DIAPERS, DISPOSABLE INCOME, DMZ, DO-IT-YOURSELF, DOUBLETHINK, D
SHELTERS, FAMILY ROOM, FAST FOOD, FAX, FILTER-TIPPED CIGARETTES, FIRST STRIKE, FLYING SAUCER, FOOD
GETTING CAUGHT, GI BILL, GOING ALL THE WAY, GRASS, GROUND ZERO, GUIDED MISSILE, GUILT BY ASSOCIATION, HAPPY-GO
INFRASTRUCTURE, INTERSTATE HIGHWAY, IPANA, IRON CURTAIN, JETLINER, JITTERBUG, JUNK MAIL, JUPITER ROCKET,
LEVITTOWN, *LIFE*, LIFTOFF, LINDY, LUNAR PROBE, MANBO, McCARTHYISM, METHADONE, MIDAS MUFFLER, MILITARY INE
NAME-DROPPER, NATO, NUCLEAR REACTOR, NYLON, ORBIT, ORLON, OXYDOL, PANTY RAID, PARENTING, PATIO, PENICILLIN,
SKIRT, PORTABLE RADIO, POWER STEERING, PUSH-BUTTON WAR, RADAR SCREEN, RADIATION SICKNESS, RADIOACTIVE IOD
ROLL, ROLL-ON DEODORANT, ROOM DIVIDER, SADDLE SHOES, SALK VACCINE, SARAN WRAP, SATELLITE, SCATTER CUSHIONS,
SONIC BARRIER, SONIC BOOM, SPLIT LEVEL, SPUTNIK, SQUARE, STOCKPILE, STRONTIUM 90, STYROFOAM, SUMMIT, SUPERPO
QUILIZERS, TRANSISTOR, TUPPERWARE, TV, TV DINNER, TWO-TONE KELVINATOR, UFO, UNIVAC, VELCRO, VIDEOTAPE, V
ANN LANDERS, ANTIBIOTICS, ANTIHISTAMINE DRUGS, ANTI-MISSILE MISSILE, ARMS RACE, ASTRONAUT, ATOMIC C
BETTER DEAD THAN RED, BIKINI, BINAC, BIRTH CONTROL PILL, BRAINSTORMING, BRAINWASHING, BROADLOOM, BURGER
CINEMASCOPE, CLEAVAGE, COLD WAR, COMMIES, COMPUTER, CONSUMERISM, CONTAINMENT, CONTOUR SHEETS, COOKOUT, C
ABBY, DEEP FREEZE, DESEGREGATION, DISPOSABLE DIAPERS, DISPOSABLE INCOME, DMZ, DO-IT-YOURSELF, DOUBLETHINK, D
SHELTERS, FAMILY ROOM, FAST FOOD, FAX, FILTER-TIPPED CIGARETTES, FIRST STRIKE, FLYING SAUCER, FOOD
GETTING CAUGHT, GI BILL, GOING ALL THE WAY, GRASS, GROUND ZERO, GUIDED MISSILE, GUILT BY ASSOCIATION, HAPPY-GC
INFRASTRUCTURE, INTERSTATE HIGHWAY, IPANA, IRON CURTAIN, JETLINER, JITTERBUG, JUNK MAIL, JUPITER ROCKET,
LEVITTOWN, *LIFE*, LIFTOFF, LINDY, LUNAR PROBE, MANBO, McCARTHYISM, METHADONE, MIDAS MUFFLER, MILITARY IND
NAME-DROPPER, NATO, NUCLEAR REACTOR, NYLON, ORBIT, ORLON, OXYDOL, PANTY RAID, PARENTING, PATIO, PENICILLIN,
SKIRT, PORTABLE RADIO, POWER STEERING, PUSH-BUTTON WAR, RADAR SCREEN, RADIATION SICKNESS, RADIOACTIVE IOD
ROLL, ROLL-ON DEODORANT, ROOM DIVIDER, SADDLE SHOES, SALK VACCINE, SARAN WRAP, SATELLITE, SCATTER CUSHIONS,
SONIC BARRIER, SONIC BOOM, SPLIT LEVEL, SPUTNIK, SQUARE, STOCKPILE, STRONTIUM 90, STYROFOAM, SUMMIT, SUPERPO
QUILIZERS, TRANSISTOR, TUPPERWARE, TV, TV DINNER, TWO-TONE KELVINATOR, UFO, UNIVAC, VELCRO, VIDEOTAPE, V
ANN LANDERS, ANTIBIOTICS, ANTIHISTAMINE DRUGS, ANTI-MISSILE MISSILE, ARMS RACE, ASTRONAUT, ATOMIC C
BETTER DEAD THAN RED, BIKINI, BINAC, BIRTH CONTROL PILL, BRAINSTORMING, BRAINWASHING, BROADLOOM, BURGER
CINEMASCOPE, CLEAVAGE, COLD WAR, COMMIES, COMPUTER, CONSUMERISM, CONTAINMENT, CONTOUR SHEETS, COOKOUT, C
ABBY, DEEP FREEZE, DESEGREGATION, DISPOSABLE DIAPERS, DISPOSABLE INCOME, DMZ, DO-IT-YOURSELF, DOUBLETHINK, D
SHELTERS, FAMILY ROOM, FAST FOOD, FAX, FILTER-TIPPED CIGARETTES, FIRST STRIKE, FLYING SAUCER, FOOD
GETTING CAUGHT, GI BILL, GOING ALL THE WAY, GRASS, GROUND ZERO, GUIDED MISSILE, GUILT BY ASSOCIATION, HAPPY-GO
INFRASTRUCTURE, INTERSTATE HIGHWAY, IPANA, IRON CURTAIN, JETLINER, JITTERBUG, JUNK MAIL, JUPITER ROCKET,
LEVITTOWN, *LIFE*, LIFTOFF, LINDY, LUNAR PROBE, MANBO, McCARTHYISM, METHADONE, MIDAS MUFFLER, MILITARY IND
NAME-DROPPER, NATO, NUCLEAR REACTOR, NYLON, ORBIT, ORLON, OXYDOL, PANTY RAID, PARENTING, PATIO, PENICILLIN,
SKIRT, PORTABLE RADIO, POWER STEERING, PUSH-BUTTON WAR, RADAR SCREEN, RADIATION SICKNESS, RADIOACTIVE IOD
ROLL, ROLL-ON DEODORANT, ROOM DIVIDER, SADDLE SHOES, SALK VACCINE, SARAN WRAP, SATELLITE, SCATTER CUSHIONS,
SONIC BARRIER, SONIC BOOM, SPLIT LEVEL, SPUTNIK, SQUARE, STOCKPILE, STRONTIUM 90, STYROFOAM, SUMMIT, SUPER
TRANQUILIZERS, TRANSISTOR, TUPPERWARE, TV, TV DINNER, TWO-TONE KELVINATOR, UFO, UNIVAC, VELCRO, VIDEOTAPE,
ANN LANDERS, ANTIBIOTICS, ANTIHISTAMINE DRUGS, ANTI-MISSILE MISSILE, ARMS RACE, ASTRONAUT, ATOMIC CLOUD, AUTO